E
873
.B34

Baker, James Thomas.

A Southern Baptist
in the White House

DATE			
MAY 31 '84	OCT 16 1996	JAN 07 2005	
JAN 8 '85	MAR 0 2 1998		
APR 20 1987			
APR 20 1987	SEP 3 0 1998		
MAY 1 9 1987	DEC 2 2 1998		
OCT 1 7 1990			
JAN 3 0 '92			
FEB 1 8 '92	2000 3 2004		
NOV 2 1 '92			
MAR 15 1995	DEC 0 8 2004		

A
Southern Baptist
in the
White House

A
Southern Baptist
in the
White House

BY

JAMES T. BAKER

THE WESTMINSTER PRESS
PHILADELPHIA

BOOK DESIGN BY DOROTHY ALDEN SMITH

Published by The Westminster Press ®
Philadelphia, Pennsylvania

PRINTED IN THE UNITED STATES OF AMERICA

Library of Congress Cataloging in Publication Data

Baker, James Thomas.
    A Southern Baptist in the White House.

    1. Carter, Jimmy, 1924–   —Religion.
    2. Presidents—United States—Biography. I. Title.
    E873.B34   973.926'092'4 [B]   77–8926
    ISBN 0–664–24144–1

For Socrates—
RALPH LYNN

Contents

Preface

ANOTHER "CARTER AND RELIGION" BOOK, you say. Will they never end? Are they to be like Carters themselves—an inexhaustible supply one after another ad infinitum, ad nauseam? Yes, like Carters they will keep coming, while he is President and long after, now by journalists, then by historians and intimates. But also like Carters, while the books may appear to be the same, they will not all be just alike.

Why on earth another Carter book? Quite simply because the ones that have gone before have so totally missed the point. He is not so easy to capture.

There are the "Carter speaks" kind of books whose authors seem to think that by providing long quotations from his speeches they have captured the essence of the man. Anyone who has watched Carter speak knows that this is not true. He is teeth and hair and tone more than words. He has charisma, but he is not particularly gifted with words. Nor do his words really express him best.

There are the books that treat him as a worker of

miracles, a somewhat mysterious man who accomplished the impossible dream by winning the Democratic nomination and then the Presidency. As a political historian, and therefore something of a cynic, I find little mystery in his success. I find extraordinary self-confidence, a good sense of organization, issues, planning, and a lot of hard, dull work that began with crack-of-dawn handshaking, but no miracles.

Then there are the books that herald him as the new Christian evangelical hope, the man to fulfill conservative Protestantism's goal of reaching a lost nation with the fundamentalist gospel. As a Southern Baptist, jaded perhaps but still safely in the fold, I find him neither a true evangelical nor the harbinger of some great American evangelistic revival. A Christian, yes. More sincere about it than most, probably. A President who will try to reach certain liberal Christian social goals, possibly. But not the person to bring in the Kingdom.

As a southerner and a Baptist, yet in both cases disillusioned and removed from the mainstream enough to have some amount of perspective, I believe I can isolate and expose several of the Dixie demons that make Carter the phenomenon he most assuredly is. I was baptized and educated by his church. I lived under the Orvals and Lesters of southern demagogic infamy. My judgments on Carter may be different from those given before by Yankees and Episcopalians, but I believe they will not prove inaccurate.

Carter may not be what all his interpreters have

said, but he is indeed a remarkable man, and his story is just beginning. He will write the most important parts of it in the coming months and years. The following chapters should throw some light on what to expect and why.

J.T.B.

Chapter I

Up from the Sawdust Trail

THE FINAL NIGHT of the 1976 Democratic National Convention in New York City was very much like a Southern Baptist-sponsored, union revival meeting. And for good reason. The nominee for President, the senior evangelist of the evening, was a Southern Baptist preacher.

Jimmy Carter, nuclear submarine officer, wealthy peanut tycoon, Baptist deacon and lay preacher, had made his religious faith an issue in the primaries. He had freely and willingly discussed it in public appearances and on talk shows with newsmen who were sure at first that it would backfire on him the way George Romney's admission of being brainwashed in Vietnam had done for him in 1968. Carter had made a special point, on the Sunday before the convention opened, of attending services designed especially for him at the Fifth Avenue Presbyterian Church in Manhattan. Not since 1957, when Evangelist Billy Graham invaded Madison Square Garden for his first New York crusade, had the Big Apple been so captivated by the old-time religion.

My family and I, along with forty million other families sharing the community-expanding experience of television, watched as the revival took shape. First came the music and singing, the traditional melodies and phrases—the customary way to turn a revival congregation on. Then the Methodist-preacher's-son-turned-Presbyterian-elder Walter Mondale (a symbol of community revival cooperation, the southern version of ecumenism) stirred the worshipers with denunciations of sin in high places, of misguided mission aid programs, and of cheap grace in forgiving the unrepentant guilty, leaving the senior evangelist to take the high road of love and peace. Then came the black preacher Martin Luther King, Sr. (a further sign of community cooperation and proof that the gospel does make all men one) to give the benediction—and what a benediction! The congregation, happy, spent, sang "We Shall Overcome" and went forth into the highways and hedges to win the lost and straying. It was no surprise that *Time* magazine labeled its cover story, featuring "the team" and their comely wives, "The Democrats Reborn."

The highlight of the evening was the sermon. All political conventions, patterned after the art form created by revivalistic America, are camp meetings. All acceptance speeches are essentially evangelistic sermons that seek to capture both the moral tone and the crusading spirit of the movement they ride and perpetuate. But Jimmy Carter's sermon was the best ever.

Carter, alternating between passionate social

14

commentary and compassionate promises of mercy and reconciliation, called for 1976 to be a year of "inspiration and hope," a year in which the government would, in true Congregationalist-Baptist fashion, be given "back to the people."

America had been shaken by the problems of "a tragic war abroad and by scandals" at home, Carter said. This had disciplined and educated its people. "Guided by lasting and simple moral values, we have emerged idealists without illusions, realists who still know the old dreams of justice and liberty," he said in language that could just as well describe mature Christian citizens ready to do battle for morality and truth.

Carter invoked the great clouds of Democratic witness, the names of past leaders he was about to join in the political pantheon as his face was lifted to join theirs on the walls of the great Madison Square sanctuary: the inspirational Roosevelt, the common uncommon Truman, the dreamer Kennedy, the tragic bighearted Johnson. He looked north, south, east, and west as he listed the regional and social groups that would make up the Great Crusade to return government to the people. In recent years America has been the property of leaders wicked and weak. Moral decay has set in. We are drifting. Now "it is time for healing," for a revival of leadership. "We want to have faith again!" he declared. "We want to be proud again!"

"Unholy" alliances between politicians and money interests have conspired to shut the people out. "The tragedy of Vietnam and Cambodia, the

15

disgrace of Watergate, and the embarrassment of the CIA revelations could have been avoided if our government had reflected the sound judgment, good common sense, and high moral character of the American people," he said. Sadly it did not.

We must begin to strengthen the government closest to the people, he said. We must spend most of our money not on new weapons but on our people: "The poor, the weak, the aged, the afflicted must be treated with respect and compassion and with love." If anyone needs it stated more simply: "Love must be aggressively translated into simple justice."

On to the specifics of justice. It is time for "love-justice" in taxes, in health care, in equal economic opportunity, in law enforcement. To sum it up, "a proper function of government is to make it easy for us to do good and difficult for us to do wrong." A quotable quote.

So should things be in America. America's birth opened a new chapter in man's history. America was the first nation to dedicate itself to "basic moral principles," the most important of which is that government must gain its power from the people. Our rededication to this principle would revive our spirit and inspire the world once again. "I have never had more faith in America than I do today," Carter said. America is, in Bob Dylan's phrase, busy being born, not busy dying. The America we want is clean morally and ecologically, proud of its past and future, free, a nation that "harnesses the idealism of the student, the compassion of the nurse or social

16

worker, the determination of the farmer, the wisdom of the teacher, the practicality of the business leader, the experience of the senior citizen, and the hope of the laborer."

So let us go forward from this place to retake our government, to "embark on great national deeds." If we will, then once more as brothers and sisters "our hearts will swell with pride to call ourselves Americans."

He stopped. The great crowd cheered and sang. It had not been a logical progression of ideas. Revival sermons seldom are. It had been, rather, a series of emotional phrases lobbed one after another into the congregation.

In fact, when Carter said America is "busy being born, not busy dying," he misused Dylan's verse. Dylan's view of a "funny ol' world" is rather more pessimistic than Carter's view of America:

> Seems sick an' it's hungry, it's tired and it's torn,
> It looks like it's adyin' an' it's hardly been born.

Why Carter, who quotes the verse correctly in his autobiography, chose to revise it is not known. He probably wanted to appear both "with it" and optimistic. He obviously wants to reattract America's "lost" people to useful lives. Perhaps he sees in Dylan's poetry a means of communication with one group. He might be wise when he quotes to quote correctly. But his misuse of this verse gives us insight into his mind.

Nevertheless, the man who as a boy had listened to Democratic conventions on a radio hooked to a car battery knew how to exhort such a crowd. So did the elder Dr. King as he announced to God and mankind that Jimmy Carter was the man brought to this place at this time to bring America home again. With both men's benedictions ringing in their ears, this congregation of blacks and southern whites, low-church Protestants and thoroughly puritanized Catholics and Jews left the sanctuary to begin their Great Crusade.

It was no coincidence that this Presidential nominee would turn his convention finale into a revival meeting. Saved by grace when he was eleven years old, reared in a Baptist church, born again in his middle years, a deacon, a Sunday school teacher, a volunteer missionary, a lay preacher, a denominational leader, Jimmy Carter was, above all else, an evangelist. He had come to national attention at exactly the right time, the time prepared by what seems to be a revival of religion following the winter of our greatest discontent.

Three and a half months after that night in Madison Square Garden, in the early-morning hours of November 3, Jimmy Carter, toughened and chastened by a Presidential campaign, once again addressed the nation. His tone was softer, his words less strident. He had run up a twenty-point lead just after his convention sermon, but it had steadily declined until two days before the election his own mistakes and the inexorable power of an incumbent President had reduced him to a dead heat with.Gerald Ford. He carried his native South and the industrial states of the North, but he lost all of the Midwest and West, and it was almost three o'clock in the morning before he could claim victory.

He seemed embarrassed to win by just three percentage points (51 percent to 48 percent, or two million votes) and fifty-six (297 to 241) electoral votes. He had in general won the down-and-out vote, while Ford had won the up-and-in group. Blacks and other minorities, low-income laborers, and ethnic southerners, especially Baptists, had combined their support to make Jimmy Carter the third Baptist President, the first man from the Deep South to win that office since Zachary Taylor in 1848, the first ever to win on a personal platform which announced that the candidate had been born again.

Carter had won by gaining the votes of people who claim Jesus and people whom Jesus would probably claim were he on earth today. Yet he had lost the majority of the white vote across the nation and the overwhelming majority of the upper-middle-class vote, the vote of those who run America's businesses and local and state governments. The narrow margin of victory gave him no great mandate for change, yet the people who supported and elected him wanted and desperately needed change. He was President, but could he be the President he wanted so much to be? What kind of President would he, could he be?

The answer lies in what he is. Few people know more than the minimal, simplified facts of his life and political career. Few people fully understand his evangelical Baptist faith. Though he had campaigned for the Presidency for twenty-one months, few people had even heard of him before he began to chalk up victories in the spring primaries.

I had lived in northern Florida in 1966. The one local television station in Tallahassee shared a transmitter with the city of Thomasville just across the state line in Georgia. I saw most of the political advertising in that year's race for governor in Georgia. I even watched a debate televised state-wide between the six or eight candidates, one of which was Jimmy Carter, then a state senator. I spent most of the evening watching the antics of the comic figure Lester Maddox, the man who had closed his Atlanta restaurant rather than serve Negroes. Lester, minus his ax handles, would in 1976 be the American Independent Party's candidate for President. He would in 1966 become governor of Georgia, elected by the Georgia legislature when neither he nor Republican Bo Callaway received a majority of the popular vote in November. Carter would run third in the Democratic primary in August.

I remember Maddox. I remember Callaway. I remember ex-governor Ellis Arnall whose write-in candidacy would throw the election into the legislature. I even remember a candidate who said everyone should vote for him because he and his wife would just love to live in that new mansion in Atlanta. But I do not remember Jimmy Carter.

Neither do I remember him six years later after he had been elected governor and had led his delegation to the 1972 Democratic National Convention in

Miami. He nominated Henry Jackson of Washington for President in opposition to the "acid, amnesty and abortion" candidacy of George McGovern. But during the 1976 National Convention, when NBC replayed the tape of his nominating speech, I had trouble believing my eyes. His hair was shorter. The noisy crowd seemed impatient with the "little peanut farmer." Carter seemed uneasy and angry with the McGovern crowd. He frowned. His voice was high and shrill. He introduced "Senator Henry—Scoop—Jackson" to scattered applause. He stalked off.

It was different in 1976. His time had come. Television brought Jimmy Carter to the nation—the Georgia governor, the peanut farmer, but also the preacher.

At first the images were fleeting. He led a New Hampshire elementary class in a pledge of allegiance to the flag. He brushed snow from his hair and wished Scoop Jackson all the best as he stayed in the Senate after Carter became President. He used his second language, a swamp-celtic, rhophobic southern accent, to tell southern supporters, "Down in Fla'da, we gon' git onta ol' George Wallace, an' we gon' whoop 'im." He spoke of ethnic purity, then apologized to Papa King, then won Pennsylvania. He took on a coalition of old pros fronted by Young Galahad Jerry Brown and beat them. He put to rest fears of his Southernness—translated racist, obscurantist, dumb; his fuzziness —to Carterize came to mean to "come down foursquare on both sides of every issue"; and his salva-

21

tionist religion. The born-again Southern Baptist would be nominated for President in the Big Apple. He would be elected in November.

The campaign was hectic for everyone. First, on August 29, Carter gave his honest opinion about a pardon for draft evaders before a Seattle convention of the American Legion. Then came partial revelations about a supposedly profane *Playboy* interview. Then he was too nice and too mean in Debates I and II. On Sunday before the election (appropriately Halloween) his local church in Plains closed its doors and canceled services rather than allow a rabble-rousing black minister to worship with the congregation.

Yet Carter won, despite all the revealing mistakes, and a born-again Baptist lay preacher is the thirty-ninth President. Yet very few people know who he is and what his religious faith, so important to him, so important now for the nation, really means.

Nations, unlike calendars, begin centuries on the anniversaries of important political events. America's most significant event, the writing of the Declaration of Independence in 1776, makes each '76 the beginning of our centuries. Our third century, then, is brand-new. So too is the kind of President we have. He is new because he is southern, because he won by making himself the major issue in the campaign, and because he ran as a born-again Christian.

It still seems slightly unsettling to think that a southerner (L.B.J. was a westerner) could be elected President in his own right. None has been since the Civil War. For years after 1865 southerners were considered traitors, rebels, hardly Americans at all. Even after fifty years had passed, when Democrats began nominating them occasionally for vice-president as a reward for the votes of the solid Democratic South, no one could seriously believe that one of them—with their anti-Washington biases—could be trusted to run the country. From the 1950's on through the 1960's, as a result of the way most southern politicians reacted to the civil rights movement even the Democrats refused to put one on a national ticket.

Then something happened. George Wallace was shot. Racial integration, supported by responsible southern leaders, began to work better in the South than integration in the North. Tensions in the South cooled while they heated up in the North. Jimmy Carter, a southern racial liberal, was able to offer a somewhat embarrassed and bewildered nation some hope. Even the typically "southern" traits he still exhibited, the anti-Washington bias, the emphasis on warm, sometimes sticky human values, the full personal acceptance of history as essentially tragic, all made sense to many Americans outside the South for the first time.

In 1960, Prof. C. Vann Woodward, a historian of the South, began an article and then a book in which he tried to explain why the South was so at odds with the rest of America. He found the answer in the South's history. Its history, first slavery and then military defeat followed by grinding poverty, was

23

tragic. For most other Americans, history was a story of continual success: victory in wars, growing affluence, increasing freedom. For southerners, history is defeat, continuing poverty, deepening oppression.

The 1960's and 1970's have changed America. The majority of Americans have now been forced to see America lose a war, to see the poverty of men and of the machine age they once believed in, to see the oppression of their own agencies of social control. Jimmy Carter, whose roots are in the South, whose philosophy was molded by the South's peculiar angels and demons, now America's, who rose above defeat, poverty, and oppression, offered his services to America in 1976. America said yes to him.

Not everyone in America of course. As noted before, most of affluent America still preferred to see life the way Gerald Ford saw it. There was still evidence of a great deal of anti-southern prejudice in the national press and mass media. Billy Carter, the new President's beer-drinking brother, was probably right when in his cups on election night he accused "you television people" of being against the Georgian in the race. Certainly Carter's "ethnic purity" statement was more minutely analyzed and criticized than similar statements by Henry Jackson and Morris Udall, both certified liberals.

Harper's Magazine, a prominent bastion of American sophistication, seemed especially anxious to hurt Carter. An article in the September issue by Johnny Greene, entitled "The Dixie Smile," sought to make Carter simply a bit better camouflaged version of the typical southern politician, a Kissin' Jim Folsom with his fly zipped. Governor Folsom of Alabama, Greene reported, once urinated on New York Governor Averell Harriman's leg. "I was just livin' out a southern dream," he supposedly explained. Carter, ran the implication, was doing the same thing by fuzzing issues and pulling the wool over Yankee eyes with honest-looking smiles and claims of a new birth. Tom Watson encouraged lynching, George Wallace encouraged segregation, and Jimmy Carter encourages ethnic purity. It's all basically southern, and it has to be bad.

But most Americans do not read *Harper's*, and Jimmy Carter, an American leader because of and not in spite of his Southernness, was elected. He was elected also because of and not in spite of making himself the major issue of the campaign.

This is usually not the way to win a Presidential election. Senator Everett Dirksen of Illinois used to say that most people vote against rather than for a candidate. Usually the one they vote against is the one they know the most about, as Richard Nixon learned from bitter experience in 1960, 1962, and 1968. The longer he was before the public, the more they saw him, the more they talked about him, the more they voted for his opponent. Richard Reeves of *The New York Times* has noted that candidates for President lose by large margins only when their personal ability to govern, their administrative competence, is questioned, as with Goldwater in '64 and McGovern in '72. Since most candidates have deficiencies, weaknesses that might well call their competency into question, it is best not to let oneself become the major issue. Carter not only let himself be the major issue; he planned and carried out his wish to be. For him, as for few others before him, it worked.

It has always been a part of the southern political style, its innate personalism borrowed most probably from southern evangelism, to make oneself the major plank in one's platform. George Wallace was certainly not the only segregationalist politician in the South during the '60's; but he was the most successful with his demagoguery, so successful that he built a national following, because he personified the white resistance to racial change. What made him invincible in the South, however, generally hurt him across the country, except in places having severe racial crises. Carter, following the southern pattern, made himself the issue in 1976, but the self he presented to the American people was acceptable and by the majority of people was welcomed.

He presented himself as a man of integrity, one without taint of scandal, an outsider in national politics, an honest politician. After Watergate and its attendant loss of political faith, his primary task was to prove that he as an individual was truthful. "If I ever lie to you, if I ever mislead you," he told audiences, "please don't vote for me."

Not surprisingly, it was his honesty that the press questioned most severely. He had made honesty the issue. He had promised never to lie. His longish and sometimes involved answers to questions, his moderate, evenhanded analyses of complex issues, his open admissions of ignorance on some problems facing the nation led many commentators to suspect that he was not being completely truthful with them and with the people.

Steven Brill, again in *Harper's,* was moved to call Carter's campaign "the most sincerely insincere, politically antipolitical, and slickly unslick" of the political year. Brill recalled Carter's 1970 race for governor of Georgia in which he scored on his opponent, Carl Sanders, by labeling him organized labor's favorite boy, raked up every conceivable racial fear to counteract Sanders' popularity with blacks, and publicly proclaimed himself a redneck (sympathetic to racists) proud to run on a ticket with Lester Maddox, who was seeking to move from governor to lieutenant governor in a game of musical chairs. Since in 1976 he was running as a pro-labor, pro-black, anti-Maddox national liberal Democrat, reasoned Brill, he was in fact a liar either in 1970 or in 1976 or in both years. He had not always been a friend to blacks. He had not left Georgia financially solvent, as he claimed. He had never really shoveled peanuts, as campaign pictures showed. How could anyone believe him when he promised honest and efficient and compassionate government? His tendency to "Carterize" the issues, said Brill, was simply the "tip of an iceberg" of dishonesty. "Jimmy Carter's campaign—hungry, no philosophy, and brilliantly packaged—*is* Jimmy Carter."

Yet it appears that most Americans wanted to hear and chose to believe Carter's promise nevermore to tell a lie. They were willing, if they ever knew about them, to forgive his early indiscretions as he rose to power in a "snaky" political region. They believed him when he said he would never betray their trust. He said many times that of all previous Presidents, he admired most of all Harry Truman because he never lied; and voters recalled, perhaps with a certain amount of blind nostalgia, what they perceived as a simpler day when Presidents told it like it was. Carter told Bill Moyers in a now-famous PBS interview that he would quit his campaign if he lied during the race and that he would quit and resign the Presidency if he ever lied after being elected. This was taken by most people as a sacred pledge, an irreversible promise.

Carter admitted to Moyers that he is and always has been tenacious and competitive, but he claimed he had never deliberately hurt anyone. In speaking of his actions as governor of Georgia, he said:

> I often had to compromise, but I didn't compromise in a back room. And didn't compromise to begin with. My preference was to spell out my position openly—this is what I propose; this is the reason for it; this is the mess we have now; this is what we can accomplish—try to work harmoniously with the Legislature; try to give them all the credit they could, and then fight to the last vote.

Though the careful student of Carter's career may well find many inconsistencies and embarrassing lapses of truth, what is significant presently is that in 1976 he pledged to tell all the truth. People believed him. He is therefore bound to do so or go the way of Richard Nixon. He is a politician. He has assumed various identities to gain positions from which he could do what he thought was right. Now that he is in the ultimate political position in America, he has only history to serve, and history will judge him on the basis of his fidelity to the pledge to tell the truth. The people believed him.

They also responded favorably to a third Carter issue, his religious faith. Carter has apparently never made a secret of his church attendance and religious commitment. In the South such things help more than harm a politician, so long as they don't blind him to pragmatic principles. No one could have predicted how the claim to be a born-again Christian would be received nationwide in 1976. As it turned out, after he "went public" with it in the North Carolina primary, his popularity shot up. Critics accused him of playing politics with religion. Carter said he only answered questions honestly.

His salvation immediately roused the interest of the news media. Here was a good story: a winning Presidential candidate claiming to have had a mystical experience in which he was reborn by the grace of God through the shed blood of the Lamb: mind-boggling to the secular mind. It would be a major issue in the campaign.

Though there had been only one Roman Catholic and no Jewish President (thus thirty-seven Protestants), Carter was the first to make or let be made an issue of his evangelical salvation. He was the first serious contender with anything like a well-developed salvationist theology since William Jennings Bryan at the turn of the century. There were many writers, from David Broder to Max Lerner, who felt uneasy to alarmed by Carter's faith, particularly by its mystical and possibly messianic connotations. There was little concern for Morris Udall's lapsed but formative racist Mormonism; for Gerald Ford's strange, misguided, misinterpreted Nixon-pardoning Episcopalianism; for Jerry Brown's Zen Catholicism. But then those men were losing. Carter was going to be President, unless the American people opened their eyes to see that behind that Dixie smile lay the mind of a dangerous religious fanatic.

The reason their warnings went unheeded is that they failed to take into account the vast pool of Americans who not only would understand Carter's religious experience but who would, because of it, consider him a brother. As time and primaries passed, it became ever more evident that Carter's popularity with black and white evangelicals made the difference between victory for him and defeat for the others. Catholic theologian Michael Novak and Protestant theologian Dean Kelley estimated that somewhere around forty million adult Americans claimed to have been saved. A Gallup poll put the number higher, fifty million, 34 percent of the American adult population, one third of the electorate, the core of Carter's support.

John R. Coyne, Jr., of *National Review* pointed out this tremendous evangelical power by referring to the popularity of Billy Graham's rather bland new book *Angels,* which has sold over a million and a half copies in three years. This evangelical vote was ordinarily Republican, said Coyne, but "the word is going out along the evangelical grapevine that Jimmy Carter is really one of them, and if he wins the Democratic nomination, they will turn out for him in overwhelming numbers."

Most evangelicals are indeed politically conservative and Republican, and though many left him as the campaign showed Carter moving more to the left, many stayed, especially southerners, enough to help push him over the top and make him President. Polls showed that seven of ten Americans didn't care what Carter believed theologically, but that of the three of ten who did, 75 percent favored him because of his religious convictions, specifically because he claimed to be born again. Even his liberalism they could dismiss as the natural compassion of a Christian heart, wrongheaded perhaps but still well intended. Without this electorate, especially the white part of it, Carter might well not have won.

I remember my own reaction to Carter's conversation with PBS correspondent Bill Moyers, himself once considered Lyndon Johnson's Southern Baptist preacher in the White House but now "backslidden" way up there in New York. I had known of Carter's Baptist affiliation and his claim to rebirth, but when he spoke of having attended B.Y.P.U. (Baptist Young People's Union) and of his favorite hymn "Amazing Grace," it all came home. I turned to my wife and said, "Well, for better or worse, the next President will be one of us." Some fifty million

31

Americans must have at one time or another during the year said the same thing.

But this group of Americans became one of Carter's most crucial electoral dilemmas. This fifty million alone, as loose and volatile a coalition as it was, would not have been enough for election. To this evangelical, black, southern, Baptist constituency he would have to add ethnic Catholics, Jews, organized labor, and big city bosses, all those groups a Democrat must have to be elected. For a few weeks he pulled it off. His popularity passed the 60 percent mark. But then it began to decline rapidly. Something was wrong.

By trying to spread his appeal and perhaps mute some aspects of his primary personality, he moved a bit too far from his early support. His image as well as his words fuzzed. By appealing to New York, Pennsylvania, Ohio, and California, he seemed to be less southern. By appealing to labor unions, party bosses, and political hacks, groups he had to have to win, he seemed to be less an outsider come to reform the system. By appealing pragmatically to Catholics, Jews, and secularists, promising that his religion would in no way affect his administration except to make him more responsive to the needs of people, he was no longer quite as sharply "one of us" to evangelicals.

In August he led Gerald Ford 60 percent to 39 percent. November saw the two men neck and neck at 46 percent each. Carter had run as a politically liberal evangelical. Had he been able to hold on to both liberals and evangelicals more firmly, he might have won by a landslide. Had he been less appealing to either group, he might have lost an election that most observers thought surely any respectable Democrat could win against "Nixon's party." Had he won all of one and lost all of the other, he would certainly have gone down to defeat. He did what he had to do. He won but not by much.

Carter's narrow victory might be a very good thing—both for Carter as President and for the nation he serves. The greatest mistakes of recent years (Vietnam in 1965, the Watergate cover-up of 1972–73) were made by Presidents holding overwhelming popular mandates. Carter, a narrow winner, must be careful. He may have to be a Sunday school teacher for a time before he can be an evangelist again.

Chapter II

The Way of the Pilgrim

ONLY ON RARE, well-spaced occasions does religion enter prominently into a Presidential election. The theological homogeneity of American society during our first hundred years, then the careful avoidance of nominating anyone from one of the new religious minorities for another fifty, kept down controversy. Neither William Jennings Bryan's evangelicalism nor William Howard Taft's Unitarianism made much of a splash. Not until 1928, when the Democratic Party, depending for victory on the new ethnic minorities, nominated the Roman Catholic Al Smith, did religion figure boldly in a race. Smith lost.

The second time it did, a recent occurrence, was when another Catholic, John Kennedy, was nominated by the Democrats. Then it was mainly evangelicals, not just Anglo-America in general, that raised the cry against papal plots. In 1976, Roman Catholics, while not terribly attracted to or impressed by Carter's evangelicalism, were far less visibly terrified of him than secularists who knew little about his faith.

The Carter and Kennedy religious flaps had certain items in common. The built-in support and the built-in opposition that each man's faith brought him were about the same. The loyalty of each man's religious community probably helped win the Presidency, although this loyalty probably cost each man votes in the other camp, and at least some members of the communities voted against "their man" for economic reasons. Each man could and to some extent did—Kennedy more than Carter—turn the religious issue against the opposition by claiming that anyone who voted against a man because of his religion was a bigot. The major difference between the two campaigns is that while the issue of religion was forced on Kennedy, Carter freely and purposely helped to make it an issue in 1976.

It first surfaced during the North Carolina primary in March. Carter was by then an affirmed winner in the North, where he had led a clogged field of liberals, and in the South, where he had achieved something of a political miracle by defeating George Wallace in Florida. The news media immediately made his public confession of faith a big story, and within a month *The New York Times* could say flatly that the issue had helped more than hurt the Carter campaign. Dean Kelley, author of *Why Conservative Churches Are Growing*, told people who wrote him and were hungry for deeper analysis of the strange phenomenon that Carter's belief in a personal God who speaks to his children is not only acceptable but preferred by forty to fifty million Americans. Catholic religious writer Michael Novak said: "There is a hidden religious power base in American culture which our secular biases prevent many of us from noticing. Jimmy Carter has found it."

Indeed he had. It was so powerful and brought Carter such support in the polls that Gerald Ford, an unelected President with a dogfight on his hands just to win his own party's nomination for a term of his own, began scraping together his minor claims to be an evangelical. An Episcopalian, he appeared before the Southern Baptist Convention to remind them that his ministerial son had attended one of their colleges; and he assured a convention of National Religious Broadcasters that he was indeed of the evangelical persuasion. He reminded newsmen that he prayed and read his Bible daily. He described in some detail a recent experience in which he had met God personally, and his son later identified it as a rebirth. He made a point of having Billy Graham stop by for White House chats and of stopping off at Graham's alma mater, Wheaton College, for a major address. He attended the First Baptist Church of Dallas to collect the endorsement of Southern Baptist power W. A. Criswell. It was, as *Newsweek* magazine called it, "The Year of the Evangelical."

But for the three fourths of the nation and the two thirds of the electorate that had not been saved, redeemed, born again, or whatever word is used to describe low-church Protestantism's emphasis upon a personal confrontation with God through Christ, some puzzlement lingered. They might like

Carter's ideas or his smile or his southern accent, but they hadn't the faintest notion what all the theological jargon meant. For them it was—and doubtless still is—as strange as it was and is familiar to all the various kinds of evangelicals.

Salvation in its simplest traditional Christian terms means being healed, having the gap between God and man healed by an experience in time and space of reconciliation. Its theology presumes that when mankind in Adam fell from God's grace and was separated from his uninterrupted presence, God began preparing the way for reconciliation, healing, salvation, through his Son and anointed one Jesus Christ. Salvation is, then, a much more precise experience than, say, Rousseau's healing, his sudden realization of union with nature, in Lake Geneva. It is a deed planned and carried to fulfillment by God. It is done through the vicarious death of Christ.

To be fair and honest with the cynic, it does tend to occur most regularly among those trained by salvationist churches to expect it. It is also most common in those wrestling with ego and ambition and even with security: children seeking to earn the adult world's respect, sexually ripening adolescents, runaway teen-agers, menopausic men and women (e.g., Charles Colson, Eldridge Cleaver, Jimmy Carter) facing crises in their lives. They turn to God for help. They are saved as their "teacher" tells them they will be. They call it rebirth. It is a perfectly natural experience in which God fills perfectly natural needs. It is calling upon God and

37

being answered. It is God calling and a person responding.

To be born again is theologically essentially the same thing as being saved. Jesus used the term "be born again" when visited by a Jewish religious leader, Nicodemus (John 3:7). Brushing aside the man's introductory compliments, Jesus told him that if he wanted to see God's Kingdom he must be born again. When the elderly man showed signs of confusion, Jesus explained that he was referring not to physical birth, by which a man is born into this world, but spiritual birth, in which one is born into the Kingdom, the Kingship of God. Again comes the idea that this event is a healing of the spirit, a reconciliation with God. Again it seems perfectly natural, if not universal.

This passage of Scripture and others like it dealing with rebirth and salvation were given less and less attention or interpreted in slightly different ways as the Middle Ages passed. According to a recent Gallup poll, only one in five American Roman Catholics, even in this Protestantized nation which has Billy Graham on all three networks, claims this experience of rebirth. Salvation for Catholics came to be and apparently, to a great degree, still is the total collective benefit of partaking continually in sacraments provided man by God through Christ through the church, a series of tiny graces that at death precipitate the full, final grace.

It was in burgeoning, radical Protestantism after 1500 that the experience of rebirth at one moment in a confrontation with God, not necessarily with human aid, began to be stressed as a possibility, a necessity for all. The "lower" the Protestant movement, the farther from traditional Catholicism, the greater the emphasis on this experience. John Wesley, the founder of Methodism, had the experience. So did the leaders of most of the American Protestant churches. These Protestants said they got their authority for this mode of salvation from taking seriously the message of the gospel, in Greek the *euangelion,* and this is why they are called evangelicals.

Thus salvation is often stereotyped as a low-church Protestant phenomenon, cultically limited to Methodists and their unacknowledged Holiness stepchildren, "Wesleyan" Baptists and Presbyterians, and all sorts of wild, exotic sects. Despite Gerald Ford's protestations, it is believed to be alien to Roman Catholic and other "high" church liturgical fellowships.

This last is not necessarily true. In her recent book *Drama of Salvation,* the Catholic writer Rosemary Haughton says that the great gulf between Catholic and Protestant salvation, a gulf she believes was created by Catholic and Protestant theologians during the Reformation, is a false definitional dichotomy. Those men, she says in this day of ecumenism, were simply looking for differences to exploit. While Protestants pushed leftward to claim that salvation is only the single event which sets a person permanently on the road to heaven, Catholics leaned heavily backward to claim that salvation is only the final reward at death for a life of virtue achieved through sacramental grace. Neither side gave an inch. Neither admitted the truth of the other. It was not an age of toleration.

But Ms. Haughton and many others, Protestants and Catholics, now admit the complementary nature of the two definitions. Catholicism, she says, has always taught Protestant salvation too! It may not be as common. It may not happen to everyone. It may be considered more unusual than in Protestantism. But just as Protestants now see that salvation is indeed a final reward as well as a mid-life event, so Catholics see that salvation for some is indeed a miraculous event. It makes saints. It attracts millions to Lourdes and Fatima.

The late Catholic poet-monk Thomas Merton told in his autobiography, *The Seven Storey Mountain,* several experiences with God which Protestants might take for salvation. Once in Rome after a day studying church art, once in Greenwich Village when a "Stranger" asked him for money and he realized God had sent it as a test, and once while praying for direction in life he heard chapel bells calling him home—six hundred miles away—these were all mystical experiences with God, experiences of salvation. They might not satisfy every Protestant's qualifications for rebirth—some indeed say it can happen only once—but then evangelical Protestants can't always agree among themselves about when and how it happens. Other Catholic holy men and women have recited such experiences. They are considered special, but in no way unnatural, abnormal, or un-Catholic.

It is not belief or disbelief in miracles or in experiences of the immediate presence of God that differentiates Catholic or liturgical salvation from Protestant or evangelical salvation. It is evangelicalism's insistence that this special experience is necessary for anyone who wants to be saved for heaven. Evangelical theology claims that unless a person has consciously "accepted Christ," he is not saved, reborn, or even a Christian, no matter how many sacraments he has received.

What makes defining evangelical theology difficult is that unlike Catholicism it has no central authority and thus no clear unity. Different traditional evangelical communities disagree on various points, even on the meaning and method of salvation. Some lean much closer to the sacraments and liturgy than others. Some believe salvation comes more slowly, in installments as it were, while others believe it is immediate, once for all. Confusing the picture even more are the new groups that have recently risen and have appropriated, sometimes inappropriately, the name and terminology of traditional evangelicalism. It is among these groups that Carter's early appeal faded in the homestretch. Those groups in the South he kept because of the ethnic preference for "one of us." Those in the Midwest and Far West he generally lost.

Neo-evangelicalism as opposed to traditional, denominational evangelicalism sometimes stands for warmed-over fundamentalism with its old intolerance for those who do not accept its interpretation of doctrine. It sometimes today covers for charismatic groups who exclude persons whose rebirth is not accompanied by "signs of the Spirit," such as speaking in tongues, faith healing, and other manifestations. Originally intended to denote inclusiveness—to welcome all people to share the experience that only a few could share in other faiths—evangelicalism sadly today sometimes denotes movements that claim exclusive rights to God. Attempts of young people in some of these groups to moderate the chilling or scalding elements, to speak for less strident orthodoxy, more social involvement, a more ecumenical spirit, have in most places met with severe opposition and their efforts have resulted in division.

Jimmy Carter can accurately be identified as an evangelical. He believes in the gospel. He has been saved. He is born again. But he is a Southern Baptist, a specific kind of evangelical. The Southern Baptist Convention, a denomination of some twelve million people, has consistently refused to join either the liberal ecumenical National Council of Churches or the conservative National Association of Evangelicals. Foy Valentine, of the Southern Baptist Christian Life Commission, has said: "We are *not* evangelicals. That's a Yankee word. They want to claim us because we are big and successful and growing every year. But we have our own traditions, our own hymns, and more students in our seminaries than they have in all of theirs put together. We don't share their politics or their fussy fundamentalism, and we don't want to get involved in their theological witch-hunts." Mr. Valentine should not leave the impression that we Southern Baptists have no conservative political views, no abiding, chaffing fundamentalism, and no theological witch-hunts. We do. We just want to keep them our own. They threaten our fragile coalition so much that we can't afford to let them get out of hand. Too close association with the chilly intellectual or red-hot charismatic neo-evangelicals might well be fatal for us.

Jimmy Carter is more a Southern Baptist than any other kind of evangelical and certainly more so than a neo-evangelical. He exhibits no mean theological spirit, no signs of the Spirit. As neo-evangelicals learned this, they melted away to vote their pocketbooks. Carter said that as President he would attend a local Washington Baptist church (just as his daughter, Amy, would attend a local public school) and not make a big show of having big-name preachers come to the White House for services. He has since become a member of Washington's First Baptist Church.

Southern Baptists are the southern branch of the American Baptist denomination descended from a seventeenth-century British nonconformist sect that originally had little distinctive theology except to require adult participation in two sacraments: Baptism and the Lord's Supper. Only adults could be baptized (later Southern Baptists came to require full immersion) and actively participate in ecclesiastical celebrations because the Baptists believed that a person must be consciously aware of what he is doing to satisfy God's requirements of

43

free will. For their other doctrines, since they were generally simple people and boasted few theologians and since they did not believe in written creeds, they permitted great latitude; but eventually they settled on an unwritten body of theological principles that reflected an almost perfect blend of the two great strains of Protestant thought: Augustinian Calvinism and Armenian Wesleyism. True to the former, salvation comes as an act of God, a call from God for man to return to his Maker; true to the latter, each person has the free will to accept or reject this reconciliation.

According to Baptists, all who are truly saved have had this experience of rebirth. With some it was gradual; with others it was sudden, blinding; but the opportunity comes to all. This makes the Baptist faith quite democratic—appropriate for America it would seem—and personally demanding. Each person must judge his own salvation, and he should not be baptized and participate in church membership unless he is sure it has come.

Salvation, for Baptists, comes by responding to conviction at hearing the Word preached. It is usually accompanied by great emotion. When it occurs in childhood—and it does so more often today in our society where the young seem to mature faster—it is quite often followed in later years by one or more further, often much deeper experiences that Baptists tend to explain in one of two ways: (1) as a sign that the person was not in reality saved in childhood, in which case he is rebaptized; (2) or as an indication of a return to or a deepening of faith, in which case he makes a public rededication of his life to Christ. This is the reason that Southern Baptists count as equally important the rededications and new conversions in each year's revival meeting. Since salvation is supposed to be "once for all" and yet its manifestations obviously come many times, it is important that the rededication be honored and given a place in worship to keep it from being seen as a second salvation experience. Some Baptist theologians have suggested that since Baptist salvation theology fails to fit psychological reality, we should compare rebirth not to the moment when an infant leaves the mother's body but to the moment when the child becomes fully human, when he recognizes his individuality and responsibility, the end result of many steps in growing. So far such ideas have been slow to catch on.

Salvation for Baptists, especially these later, second or third manifestations, *can* lead—though Southern Baptists generally discourage it as tastelessly Pentecostal—to signs of the Spirit, such as faith healing and speaking in tongues. This would lead us to think for a moment about the strange but not unique career of Jimmy Carter's sister, Ruth Carter Stapleton.

Of Lillian Carter's four children, only brother Billy seems never to have "caught" religion, though some perversity in me calls him the most truly, honestly religious of the lot. The other three, Jimmy and his sisters Gloria and Ruth, are good Southern Baptists, baptized as children and saved again—Baptist orthodoxy says revived—in adulthood. Of the three saved Carters, Ruth is by far the most theologically vocal. She is in fact a preacher.

Ruth and her husband, a North Carolina veterinarian, have formed a nonprofit organization, Behold, to pay her travel expenses to speaking engagements all over America and in such foreign countries as Indonesia, Japan, and England. She claims to have been a participant in sessions that healed the deaf, the lame, and the congenitally diseased.

In her modest-sized book, *The Gift of Inner Healing*, and a set of tapes to go with it, she describes herself as a sheltered, spoiled young lady who at nineteen found herself married and out in a cold world without Daddy's protection from terrors like adult responsibility and childbirth. Soon after the birth of her fourth child in 1959, she experienced black moods that left her desperate for help. A near-fatal car accident forced her to realize that she wanted very much to die. She took group therapy, then attended an interdenominational retreat of neo-Pentecostals. She lived three months alone in a mountain cabin and returned for a second retreat at the lodge. There at last she received "the baptism of the Holy Spirit" through the laying on of hands and at a later time spoke in tongues.

After graduate work in psychology at the University of North Carolina, she set to work organizing a program to spread her ideas about spiritual healing. With a technique that combines elementary psychology and religious inspiration, she invites her clients to relive bad, hidden memories that may be causing present trauma. As they relive the memories, she asks her clients to imagine Jesus there, forgiving everyone, reconciling alienations, removing spiritual scar tissue. She claims only to replace the "negatives" of fear, frustration, inferiority, guilt, and loneliness with the "positive" of Christ's love.

Perhaps her most important "case" was her brother Jimmy. In 1966 he had just been defeated in his first race for governor of Georgia. He was discouraged. He asked his little sister to go for a walk in the woods with him. She convinced him that he would never be happy until, like her, he made Jesus the most important thing in his life. They prayed. No one knows what else they said, whether they discussed the scars caused by the father who spoiled Ruth and bullied Jimmy, but it is acknowledged by both of them to have been an important event in Carter's spiritual pilgrimage. Carter, perhaps knowing how far Ruth exceeds the bounds of orthodox Baptist and American religious taste, tends to credit it less than Ruth; but he does admit that it was a step toward his adult rebirth.

Jimmy Carter was baptized, by full immersion, in his twelfth year, at the end of a Baptist revival meeting in which he had one night responded to the visiting evangelist's invitation to trust Jesus. But it was not until he was forty-two, the year he lost his bid for the governor's mansion, that he began to think of a faith deeper than teaching Sunday school and organizing district Brotherhood suppers. He told Bill Moyers:

> I was the Chairman of the Board of Deacons. I was the head of the Brotherhood in all the 34 churches in my district, and head of the Finance Committee, and Sunday school teacher just about all my life. I thought I was really a great Christian.

> And one day the preacher gave this sermon—I don't remember a thing he said—I just remember the title —"If you were arrested for being a Christian, would there be any evidence to convict you?"

> And my answer by the time that sermon was over was "No." I never had really committed myself totally to God—my Christian beliefs were superficial. Based primarily on pride, and—I'd never done much for other people. I was always thinking about myself, and I changed somewhat for the better. I formed a much more intimate relationship with Christ. And since then, I've had just about like a new life.

Carter says elsewhere that it was in 1967, perhaps a year after his defeat, the sermon, and his walk with Ruth but still in the post-election-letdown period, as a man just turned forty and failed, that he had *the* experience in which he fully committed himself to Christ and found the inner assurance that transformed his life. The next year, 1968, he volunteered two weeks of the month of November to work in an evangelistic crusade in Springfield, Massachusetts. Since he spoke Spanish, he was teamed with a Cuban-American Baptist pastor named Eloy Cruz, who is mentioned prominently in Carter's book *Why Not the Best?* and who still remembers Carter's contribution to the crusade. The quiet, unemotional experience of committing himself to Christ had led to healthy service to his church.

Catholics might wonder what he was doing in Massachusetts trying to make Baptists out of Spanish-speaking Americans, but he was simply supplying aid to a project that his church considered legitimate, and arguments should probably be addressed to the missionary-minded Southern Baptists instead of to Carter.

Carter's salvation then, early and late, is as healthy and positive as anyone could ask—even a strict Southern Baptist. He is, in fact, the epitome of the enlightened Southern Baptist. His faith has given him inner peace without neutralizing his ambition to secular service. It has helped him to arrive at compassionate liberalism without making him lose touch with the kind of people who elect politicians. It has caused him to deepen his theological understanding by reading Reinhold Niebuhr and Paul Tillich. Jimmy Carter is, in short, the very best Southern Baptist that religion and culture can offer.

Thus salvation and rebirth. Jimmy Carter is only one of millions of Americans who claim personal transformation through experiences with God. Quite a large number of those recently making such a claim are public figures, among them a disproportionate number of politicians. Are they sincere, or are they taking advantage of the current wave of religious revival that Evangelists Billy Graham and

Oral Roberts have predicted for the past twenty-five years? Is the Harold Hughes type of "professional men for Christ" movement bearing fruit, or do politicians see in public confessions of faith good camouflages for failure to serve the public trust? Did Gerald Ford sincerely want to share with the people the faith that Evangelist Billy Zeoli shared with him, or was he simply trying to hide a record of weak political vision behind religious curtains? Was Charles Colson, a Nixon aide convicted of obstructing justice, really and truly born again (*Born Again,* the name of his book), or did he see in salvationism a way to get early release from prison, and a lecture tour to regroup his personal finances? Such disturbing questions abide.

Talk of religion can cover a multitude of political sins. Spiritualism can turn minds from their duty to help make secular America a better place. Charles Colson, for example, lumps Nixon's flights into the Wild Red Yonder with Lyndon Johnson's Great Society social legislation to try to prove that all political efforts at making the world better are doomed to failure. Only when we get everyone saved can we expect things to improve. No need to try anything else.

Rebirth of course does make individuals better. It has apparently done a thing or two for Colson. At least he is no longer the kind of man that Special Prosecutor Leon Jaworski, who listened to all the Watergate tapes, called Nixon's sleaziest companion. But it does not necessarily follow that any politician who claims to have been born again, who has walked the sawdust trail, who attends prayer break-fasts, will be good for the country. If his rebirth makes him more compassionate, if it teaches him to love his people as Christ loved him, so much the better; but we must be careful as voters to make sure it has had that effect.

Richard Nixon, writing for *Decision* magazine in November 1962, recalled his own rebirth.

> I remember vividly the day just after I entered high school, when my father took me and my two brothers to Los Angeles to attend the great revival meetings being held there by the Chicago evangelist, Dr. Paul Rader. We joined hundreds of others that night in making our personal commitments to Christ and Christian service.

Richard Nixon was saved. He was publicly religious. As our youthful vice-president from 1953 to 1961, he spoke to more religious gatherings than any other politician did. He consistently spoke of his devout Quaker mother and Methodist father. Yet his record as President, despite some impressive foreign affairs achievements, is one spattered with profanity, corruption, and benign neglect of people who do not wear $400 suits. Salvation, or at least the claim to it, does not solve public problems or make a politician a statesman.

Anyone who identifies statesmanship with com-passion for the needy, with attempts to use the pub-lic wealth for the public good, may well question the validity of salvationism. Evangelicals are historically identified with political conservatism. Albert Me-nendez, in his *Religion at the Polls*, has shown, for

51

example, that evangelicals have never given a majority of their votes to a Democratic nominee. He is presumably talking primarily of northern and midwestern evangelicals, since southern evangelicals, needing governmental aid more, have generally voted Democratic. He is also talking of white evangelicals, although it can be argued that the black evangelical message—denial of the flesh, emphasis on the world to come—helped hold back the civil rights movement for a generation or more.

There is indeed a recurring and somewhat suspicious coalition today between the neo-evangelical movement and capitalist aspirations. The neo-evangelicals tend to be men of wealth and the politicians favorable to them who do tend to profit when people are lulled into otherworldly concerns by spiritualism. Oral Roberts is a wealthy man. Billy Graham, like Billy Sunday before him, spends a great deal of time in the company of men powerful and wealthy and anxious to underwrite his crusades. It would seem that religion's greatest danger is that it might live up to Karl Marx's accusation that it is the opiate of the people.

Jimmy Carter, a born-again Southern Baptist, a self-acknowledged redneck who fights for the underdog, a racial liberal, a pro-labor Democrat, just might be the man to head off such a tragic end to religion. A compassionate social activist and a born-again believer all in one, he might be able to prove at long last that Christ came to give hope to this world here and now and associate with the down-and-outs more than the up-and-ins. He might demonstrate to all the world the dual role of the born-again Christian: to love God and man.

Carter's personal theology, as told to Bill Moyers, runs to such an understanding:

> God created us in his own image, hoping that we'd be perfect, and we turned out to be not perfect but very sinful. And then when Christ was asked what are the two Great Commandments from God which should direct our lives, he said, "To love God with all your heart and soul and mind, and love your neighbor as yourself." So I try to take that condensation of the Christian theology and let it be something through which I search for a meaningful existence.

Not a bad witness! He further told Moyers that his faith makes him love other people:

> When I stand on a factory shift line . . . everybody who comes through there—when I shake hands with them, for that instance, for that instant, I really care about them.

A man who defines love as he did in his acceptance speech as "simple justice" might just be the American politician who can bring together flesh and spirit.

Some people have found Carter's faith frightening. Martin Marty of *The Christian Century* expressed early fear of a President who believed God talks to him personally and might direct him to do something humanly illogical. Malcolm Boyd warned that Carter might have a messiah complex. The fact is, however, that Carter is not a radical salvationist. He is pragmatic enough to have been elected governor of Georgia and President of the United States. His faith is not antirational or self-indulgent or coldly conservative. It has simply touched his personal life, releasing, he says, a flow of love for others.

Critics would be hard pressed to find this impeachably offensive. Compassionate evangelicals should rejoice.

Chapter III

As the Twig Is Bent—

IN THE SOUTH, where the Bible and a keen willow switch are often twin instruments of juvenile correction, a favorite philosophical injunction is, "Raise a child in the way he should go, and when he is old he will not depart from it." Jimmy Carter, with the aid of the Bible and willow switches, was raised a Southern Baptist. His father and mother—the first a conservative, the second a liberal—saw to that. He has not departed from it.

Carter was baptized and became a full participating member of a Southern Baptist church at the age of eleven. He remembers that his social life as a teen-ager in a tiny town revolved around his church. At twenty-nine he returned home from his brief naval career to settle down and become a Southern Baptist Sunday school teacher and then a Southern Baptist deacon. It was through Southern Baptist worship and missionary work that he experienced his "second grace" in 1966–67. He is therefore about as Southern Baptist as a person can be. He is, for better or worse, a Southern Baptist President.

There are a lot of Southern Baptists in the world.

Some people think there are too many; Southern Baptists generally say there are too few. They are mostly in the southern part of the United States, as the name indicates, but since World War II they have spread also into the mountains and deserts of the Southwest, mingled with the fermenting elements of the California Gold Coast, invaded the industrial cities of the Great Lakes, and even crept quietly into the Catholic citadels of the Northeast. They are now in every state of the union.

They number something like twelve million souls. They are still growing—a veritable phenomenon among the older "established" churches, most of which are hustling just to stay even. Yet they are still, despite their size and strategic location, their constant growth and unity amid near-fatal disputes, little known and even less understood by non-Southern Baptists. They remain virtual strangers on the American religious and now political scene, oddities, objects of scorn or grudging admiration, but seldom of serious study.

Why is this so? Why has a church so large as to be a socially and historically and theologically significant factor in modern American life not been hailed to the couch and diagnosed the way other large and easily identifiable churches have been? Why Roman Catholics and Jews and Mormons but not Southern Baptists? Perhaps it is because Southern Baptists have kept themselves separated from the mainstream movement of American religion. Whatever the reason, such neglect cannot continue long now that Jimmy Carter is President.

Carter is the third Baptist President. The first, Warren G. Harding of Ohio, was elected in 1920 on the promise to return America to "normalcy," a word he coined to describe America's traditional style of isolated life before the Democrat Woodrow Wilson got us involved in World War I. A Republican, Harding died in office in 1923, just as his scandal-ridden administration was beginning to collapse under the harsh light of Congressional investigations. The second Baptist President, a Democrat, the first *Southern* Baptist, was Harry Truman of Missouri. Elected vice-president with Franklin Roosevelt in 1944, he succeeded to the Presidency when F.D.R. died in office in 1945. He presided over the post-World War II conferences which molded the world of today. He was elected to his own term in 1948.

Neither of these men, however, made much of his Baptist affiliation. They were not thought of as Baptist Presidents. Jimmy Carter does and is. The Baptist, particularly the Southern Baptist, faith will be prominently discussed during Carter's years in the White House. So let us begin.

A young Southern Baptist minister, recently graduated from the seminary and serving his first church, once asked the members to suggest sermon topics. He explained to them that he wanted to answer questions that concerned them, a departure from the traditional Southern Baptist ministerial practice of preaching what God gives one to preach. He received several requests, but the most interesting and revealing came from a lady who wrote, "Will you please tell us what, if anything, happened in the church between Saint Paul and Martin Luther."

This lady's question, strange as it might seem, would not be considered odd or amusing by most Southern Baptists. Since their church's history really begins in the seventeenth century and they believe that all written authority for matters of faith was completed by the end of the first century, the fourteen hundred years between Paul and Luther are generally neglected in Baptist preaching and education. At best, the late Roman Empire and the Middle Ages are considered transitional; at worst, they are considered years of flagrant apostasy.

Luther, they believe, pointed the way back to the true faith. Calvin and Wesley moved even closer. Then the Baptists recaptured the true essence of first-century Christian faith and practice. Some Southern Baptists even believe that all through the Middle Ages, while heresy reigned, little cells of "Baptists" remained true to the simple gospel story. What Luther and Calvin and the other reformers did was to create geographical space in which these underground cells could come out into the sunlight and begin to grow. With the rise of the Baptists, the true faith once again started its march toward victory.

Modern Southern Baptists, the southern branch of the Baptists who came to America in the seventeenth century, are descended from Baptists of England and the European Rhineland, who themselves emerged from the Anabaptist movement in Holland and Germany in the mid-sixteenth century. The Anabaptists, various and sundry radical sects espousing various and sundry theologies, surfaced in the wake of Luther's stormy revolt against and break with the Roman Catholic Church in 1521. Luther and the other early reformers, who became more and more conservative as they grew older, generally despised these Anabaptists who flourished in the greater freedom they themselves had helped bring about. These variously colored and shaped sects were, as one American historian has called them, the reformers' unwanted stepchildren.

The reformers called Anabaptist any sect that was neither Catholic, Anglican, Lutheran, nor Calvinist, any group that did not belong to the large national, geographical units. The term "Anabaptist" means in simplest definition "those who baptize again," and it came from one of the groups, the one directly related to later Baptists, that required their new members to be rebaptized even though they had been baptized in one of the established churches as infants. But not all Anabaptist sects required this, and they differed on most other theological subjects as well. Anabaptist groups were the forerunners of such diverse contemporary religious denominations as Unitarians, Quakers, and of course Baptists, Southern Baptists among them.

The distinctively Baptist Anabaptists emerged in the early seventeenth century in the Rhineland and low countries of Europe and soon had churches in England as well. The English Baptists, by British crown terms "nonconformists," were early known to believe in adult baptism only and by total immersion. They depended on the New Testament for their theology. They had ordained ministers, but their church government was democratic. They were reluctant to write creeds.

Southern Baptists today still claim these early principles. Baptism is still only for adults and only by total immersion. So teaches the New Testament, they say, and so must it be. Church decisions, whether to admit a new member, increase missionary activity, or build a new sanctuary, must be brought before the entire membership for passage. There are no creeds, and no one can be penalized or reprimanded for not believing exactly what other members believe.

At times these principles are severely strained. Although no Southern Baptist church baptizes infants, a recent emphasis upon numbers, competition among churches to see who can show the greatest yearly increases, has led to the baptism of quite young children. There are no established age limits, provided the child makes a public profession of faith, and no one can say precisely when a child is responsible and therefore an adult. Jimmy Carter was baptized at the age of eleven. Many children today are baptized at age six or seven. They are all immersed. They are then able to vote with other adult members on every church matter.

Southern Baptist democracy, the form of church government that made this denomination grow so well in the fertile soil of North America, is today in some ways in decline too. It is being replaced, say Southern Baptists, by a more efficient system of oligarchies. Perhaps Southern Baptists have come to agree with Plato that democracy is the rule of the ignorant majority; maybe they have lost the will to keep a fissiparous democracy alive; but under the pressures of modern busyness they have gradually surrendered important power, locally and denominationally, to small committees. Vacuums in all forms of government seem always to be filled by those who love power; church democracy, with its planned vacuum at the top, seems to be no exception.

The Southern Baptist antipathy for creeds seems also weaker today than it was in times past. In recent years a number of theological controversies have erupted. One response to these divisive explosions has been to write more and more "confessions of our faith" that spell out, usually in very broad terms, what Southern Baptists believe. They deny that these are creeds; they say these "confessions" are simply guides to doctrine. But many insecure Southern Baptists, those who fear for their own and others' orthodoxy, take them to be much more than guides. There is every few years another movement to apply tests of orthodoxy to church members. These movements pose real threats to the Baptist tradition of freedom of conscience before God.

Other than these few principles, the Anabaptist Baptists of Europe and England tended to shy away from immutable theological doctrines. After all, they reasoned, the New Testament speaks for itself.

61

Any Christian, led by the Holy Spirit, can interpret it for himself. Since the Baptists were generally a simple people, they were slow to build schools of theology. The orthodoxy of these people was easily understood; their ministers needed little erudition. Besides, theological sophistication, as the Baptists saw from watching other denominations, led to arguments and unchristian conduct.

Baptist theology, developed as it was in slow, piecemeal fashion, has always been something of a synthesis, logical and utilitarian, of the ideas created by theologians in other denominations. Even today Southern Baptist seminary students read the writings of Lutheran, Presbyterian, Methodist, and even Catholic thinkers before they read Baptist writings. Baptists have produced few theologians of great merit. Baptist theology, however, a rich synthesis of the best the others offer, is of great merit.

The three great lights of European Protestantism are Lutheran, Calvinist, and Wesleyan. The early Baptists borrowed extensively from each one. What they borrowed was adapted to Baptist needs; though the ideas may not always be followed in their purest forms by modern Baptists, they are still recognizable.

From the Lutheran tradition the Baptists took their firm opposition to any earthly control over religion. Luther's rebellion against Rome, his denial of the pope's right to dictate religious truth to northern Germany, inspired the Baptists to deny that right to anyone, pope, king, or even Martin

Luther. They would advocate, and in America would at last get, total separation of church and state. They would say that no one on earth has authority to tell anyone else what to believe or how to worship God.

Luther also taught Baptists the way of salvation. While all Christians—Catholic and Protestant—believe that salvation comes from God, Luther was right to criticize the Roman Catholic Church for letting people think they "earned" their salvation. As a student of Greek, he pointed out that the Pauline word for salvation is not "justice" but "justification." A person is not given justice. He does not get from God what he deserves. He is forgiven, justified by grace. The Baptists followed Luther's lead. Southern Baptists still do.

How a person is given or receives salvation is another matter. The more Calvinistic Baptists tended to say, after the theological fashion of John Calvin and John Knox, that God the Great Judge decides all on his own who will and who will not be saved and that no man, whether elect or not, has anything to say about it. Salvation is a gift of God. The more Wesleyan Baptists, influenced by the free-will theology of the Methodist movement, held that salvation is offered to all and that every person must decide on his own whether to accept the gift. Baptists debated this issue for decades before at last forming another synthesis. Salvation, they finally said and still say, is indeed a gift of God. No one can earn it. Some have it and some do not, and this is indeed a mystery known only to God, but it does not indicate that some were given divine preference. Christ's death provides salvation for all. It comes to anyone who accepts it. Baptists consider it God's will for them to take the gospel to all the world. God is willing to save all, but he waits for them to accept his gift. They must first hear the Word, and the Word is carried by men.

The lives of two early British Baptists might personalize these somewhat abstract doctrines. The earliest famous Baptist was John Bunyan, author of *The Pilgrim's Progress.* Bunyan was born and lived his entire life and died in the English village of Bedford. Born in 1628, the year hostilities began heating up between Charles I and his Puritan Parliament, he died in 1688, the year of the bloodless revolution in which the Protestants William and Mary replaced the Catholic James II. It was a troubled time for England's various Christian groups.

The son of a village tinker, Bunyan was, except for theological and literary genius, a common man. He was the minister of Bedford's Baptist church until in 1660 the restored Charles II forbade nonconformists the right to preach in public. Ignoring the decree, he was arrested. When after three months' confinement he still refused to abide by the king's command—he preached every time he was released to visit his family—he was confined without leave for a period that stretched to six years. Released in 1666, he again took to his pulpit and was again jailed, once more for six years. He was at last released for good in 1672, a victim of and yet a victor over political and ecclesiastical oppression. The Baptist had won.

Another British Baptist was William Carey, the one man most responsible for the Baptist missionary enterprise around the world. A child of the English romantic era, a member of the league to abolish slavery in the British Empire, a lay theologian and preacher who admired the Wesleyan missionary zeal, Carey abandoned the strict Calvinism of his fellow English Baptists for a vision of world service. He persuaded his brothers to follow his vision.

Born in Northamptonshire in 1761, Carey was by trade a shoe cobbler. In 1792 he persuaded a group of ministers who were meeting at Kittering that God wanted him to go as a missionary to India. All people are God's elect, he argued, and God uses Christians as his messengers of hope. The ministers agreed to support him, but when a medical doctor also volunteered to go, Carey transferred the funds to him and worked his own way across. He spent the rest of his life making shoes and preaching the gospel on the subcontinent.

This then is Jimmy Carter's British Baptist heritage. Freedom of religious expression. Concern for one's fellowman. It is a proud heritage. It should be a positive influence on a President of the United States.

The Baptists never really caught on in deeply traditional Europe. Baptists there were and are, but no more than tiny minorities in any country. Not so in North America. The things Baptists stood for—individualism, freedom, democracy—captured the imagination of a people who had crossed an ocean to search for a better way of life. The Baptists, after an initial century of repression from the established churches in New England and Virginia, began to grow rapidly, and the Baptist faith eventually became one of the largest and most dominant religious forces in America.

The Baptists helped the new American republic decide for freedom of religion. Never part of the colonial establishment, they said that there should be no state church. They said that church and state should be completely separate, that the state has no right to dictate how people are to worship or what they must believe. Baptists helped write the Constitution and pass the bill of personal rights that guaranteed the freedom for which they had fought for so long. Their greatest hero, although he was actually not a Baptist as was once believed, was Roger Williams, who founded Providence Colony as a place of refuge for all who were persecuted for their faith. The Baptists believed in his principle. They helped make it a national policy.

The new land influenced and molded the Baptists as much as they influenced and molded it. Other movements, social and theological, helped make American Baptists what they became here. The movement, both social and ideological, known as Puritanism, helped make Baptists socially and ideologically conservative. The New England Puritans, descendants of Pilgrims, children of Calvin and

Knox, not only avoided "immoral" living—drinking, gambling, dancing—but worked to outlaw it in the communities where they had numerical superiority. Baptists, especially the southern branch, became quite puritan and still are today. It is hard to imagine Episcopalian or Unitarian ministers publicly condemning one of their members for granting a *Playboy* interview, but it was not at all surprising to find Southern Baptists doing so.

Another peculiarly American influence on Baptists, especially the southern branch, was the nineteenth-century revival movement. Colonial Americans, contrary to some popular opinion, were not largely affiliated with churches, and the farther from the eastern seaboard they roamed, the less they attended church at all. Thus, soon after the independence of the country, the various denominations, especially the low-church groups with less ecclesiastical restraint, began evangelizing the frontier. They were spectacularly successful. The Presbyterians, the Methodists, the Baptists held revivals that brought multitudes into their memberships. All of them, especially the Southern Baptists, were transformed by the experience.

The Southern Baptist worship service is to this day a domesticated version of the frontier camp meeting. It is built around the evangelistic sermon. The purpose of the sermon is not so much to teach as to call sinners home to God. It is not always a nourishing steady diet for growing Christians, but it continues to bring in the lost.

Southern Baptists became, as a result of the revivals, true salvationists, salvation taking on a new meaning in a new environment. Whereas they had before this time followed a Lutheran understanding that salvation is a continuing process throughout life, after the revivals they tended to see salvation as an emotional event at one point in a person's life. It was something that happened at a particular time and place, once for all. This has caused some problems for them because of adult experiences of second and third savings. It has also tended to diminish the drive to serve a needy world. If improperly interpreted, salvation can make a person selfish, interested only in his own soul or, if interested in others, interested only in their eternal salvation and not in their present physical condition. Southern Baptists are still trying to make theological adjustments to these problems.

Still another American movement to influence Baptists, Southern Baptists perhaps more than other Baptists, was the early twentieth century's fundamentalism. Fundamentalism, a theologically conservative reaction to the excesses of liberal Christian rationalism and to Christian socialism, sought to return Protestantism, by force if necessary, to traditional doctrines such as blood atonement, the physical resurrection of Jesus, and the verbal inspiration of the Bible. Moderates and liberals still ask how traditional, how truly fundamental these doctrines are, especially when applied as rigidly as the fundamentalists wanted to apply them.

Fundamentalism divided several Protestant denominations. Southern Baptists, always more conservative than most, easily surrendered to it. Southern Baptist fundamentalism, except among a few and on rare occasions, is a more easygoing, cheerful, sunnier movement than the northern variety, but fundamentalism it is. It has led to the firing of "liberal" seminary professors and to the recalling of books published by denominational presses but thought to be dangerous.

Southern Baptists, then, are on almost anyone's social or theological spectrum, well to the right of center. They are conservative morally and doctrinally. Only the rarest of individual Baptists is not.

There are in addition to these very American influences certain distinctively southern influences, elements of the southern social and religious experience, that have molded Southern Baptists. Southern Baptists, it sometimes appears, are more southern than Baptist.

The American Baptist denomination divided along geographical lines—Mason and Dixon—in the 1840's. Many issues separated them, but the most important and decisive one was slavery. Many southern Baptists owned slaves. Some even tried to take their slaves along with them to mission fields. These Baptists in the South chose to leave the northern Baptists and form their own convention. Most other Protestant denominations divided north and south in this period too, but most of them have since reunited. Baptists have not.

Southern Baptists grew to be a much larger denomination than their northern American Baptist brothers. They grew so large that they inevitably became part of the southern religious establishment. The descendants of men who died to separate church and state let themselves become a kind of unofficial state church of Dixie. They did so not by imperial decree but by becoming the kind of church that southern whites felt at home with. Negroes, who had worshiped with their masters and, after the Civil War, with other whites, were eased out and into all-black churches. During the racially turbulent 1960's, many Southern Baptist churches, Jimmy Carter's included, officially voted to exclude blacks from the sanctuary.

Southern Baptists have been crippled by their own success. They are so much a part of southern society that they cannot easily or effectively speak to it prophetically. They speak with a decidedly southern theological accent. Yet this is in another sense their greatest asset. The South is being watched by people all over the world to see if racial peace can be maintained and racial harmony achieved between two peoples so long segregated from each other. Southern Baptists, whom no one either black or white can accuse of being outsiders, who do indeed speak with a southern accent, who are as southern as they are Baptist, will inevitably play a large part in this great drama. It is quite an opportunity.

Another southern quality that helped mold the Southern Baptists is the mid-nineteenth-century movement of particularism, known among Southern Baptists as landmarkism. While it is a close cousin to similar movements in other Protestant churches north and south and even resembles the Catholic concept of apostolic succession, Southern Baptist landmarkism has a decidedly southern and Baptist flavor.

According to the landmarkists, the Baptist Church began not in the Reformation of the sixteenth and seventeenth centuries but in A.D. 33 and has continued in a long chain of blood, suppressed and persecuted but always faithful to the fundamentals of the faith to this day. The majority of Southern Baptists still believe that this is true, and it is one of the reasons they refuse to join ecumenical movements. Since theirs is the True Church and they know the Whole Truth, they need not look to other churches for advice or help. This makes them very denominational. They want to be and are self-sufficient.

So began the Southern Baptists—European, American, southern. Theirs are some of the biggest problems and greatest opportunities in the world today. They both frighten and inspire the church as a whole. They have now produced a President.

They voted for Jimmy Carter 56 percent to 44 percent. His support was even higher before he proved himself more a Democrat than a Dixiecrat and before his *Playboy* interview shocked puritan sensitivities. The South and its Southern Baptists are growing ever more Republican. They gave Richard Nixon 77 percent of their votes. Jimmy Carter, the candidate without an accent, brought them back to the Democrats by being "one of us."

The possibility of having a Southern Baptist President alarmed many people outside the South and the Baptist faith. According to Prof. Glenn Hinson of the Southern Baptist Theological Seminary in Louisville, Kentucky, this was because Southern Baptists have in recent years strayed from and let most Americans forget their positive doctrines: freedom of worship, separation of church and state, and democracy. They have instead projected an image of ultraconservatism, racism, and self-satisfied bigotry. Professor Hinson admitted, sadly it seemed, that all that most people think of when Southern Baptists are mentioned are rigid theological conservatism that preludes rejection of ecumenical exchange, overly zealous mission programs that tend to deny the validity of other faiths, and right-wing movements to "put God back in the schools," which threaten religious freedom. He warned Southern Baptists that the world would be watching them now more than ever before. He advised them to return to their roots.

Contemporary Southern Baptists, products of phases and movements, both positive and negative, over three hundred years of history, are many things. This is why they are often found working at cross-purposes with themselves. It is possible for an individual Southern Baptist, depending on his personality and knowledge of his tradition, to be almost anything. The question we should ask is, What kind of Southern Baptist is Jimmy Carter? It will be good for the country if he rejects the bad things of his faith. It will be very good for the country if he accepts and tries to live by the good.

Chapter IV

—So Grows the Tree

BEING A SOUTHERN BAPTIST is not easy. It is a heavy responsibility and a hard job. It is at once sorrow and joy. It is despair and infinite hope. A Southern Baptist is a distinctive kind of Christian. A Southern Baptist President will be a distinctive kind of President.

Many people, theologians and historians of other denominations among them, look with dread at having a Southern Baptist, especially a good one, in the White House. Since Southern Baptists as a type are dangerous, so too must be a Southern Baptist President. Southern Methodist University professor Albert Outler said during the primary campaign: "The fact is the Southern Baptists have been culturally isolated and are theologically unsophisticated. They have had no experience in dealing as equals with evangelicals who are different from themselves. They also have no basis in their theology for working politically with Catholics, Jews, and secular moralists, whom they view as unregenerated worldlings, heading for damnation unless converted. They want a society ruled by those who know what

74

the Word of God is. The technical name for that is 'theocracy,' and their Napoleon, whether he likes it or not, is Jimmy Carter."

Laying aside the questionable internal logic of Mr. Outler's statement and the fact that as the general election wore on, some leading Southern Baptists, including W. A. Criswell of Dallas' First Baptist Church, endorsed Gerald Ford, Outler's doubts about Southern Baptists and "their candidate" were probably shared by quite a large number of church watchers. Significantly it took a representative of The United Methodist Church, the Southern Baptists' only real rival for religious power and influence in the South, and one from Dallas, a city in which Baptists are thoroughly disliked by non-Baptists, to tell the truth about this animosity.

Yet not all theologians and historians of other faiths would agree with Mr. Outler. Kenneth Scott Latourette, one of Christendom's most prestigious twentieth-century historians, once wrote: "We who are its beneficiaries have reason for profound gratitude for the Baptist heritage. That gratitude is for noble spirits, many of them far from perfect, but all of them among those who are 'being saved.' Most of them were humble in the sight of the world and usually found no place in enduring human memory. Nevertheless they were great souls who dreamed and built better than they knew." Latourette was of course speaking of Baptists dead and gone, but his words could easily be applied to contemporary Baptists as well as to their ancestors and to Southern Baptists as well as to British or American or National (black) Baptists. Recent image should not blind us to the Baptist heritage and to the positive values of having one of their kind as President.

Jimmy Carter will be President before he will be a Southern Baptist President, but a Southern Baptist President he will be. Some of the things Southern Baptists believe and teach their followers could be problems for a President, depending on how he decides to interpret and apply them. Some things will actually make him a better President. We might look at the major ones and appraise each.

1. Southern Baptists are puritans. Although they do not necessarily share the early New England colonists' theology on many matters, they do follow the colonists' strict moral code. Southern Baptist ministers seldom take an active part in electoral politics, saying that church and state should be separate, but they do lead local-option fights to ban gambling, the sale of alcoholic beverages, and even commercial sales on Sunday from their districts. Times are changing, and younger Southern Baptists are noticeably more morally tolerant, but still there remains a strong puritan opposition to and guilt about fleshly indulgences.

There also remains a tendency to want to impose the strict Southern Baptist moral code on society at large. Puritanism as a Protestant phenomenon began in Geneva, where John Calvin founded his theocracy of the elect. Some are chosen by God to be saved and some are not, said the Calvinists, but all must be forced to live sane, moral lives. The

Christian majority therefore banned by law such vices as dancing and public flirtation. They required the citizens to pray before meals. They saw to it that no one worked on Sunday. Their descendants placed the same strictures on seventeenth-century England, eighteenth-century New England, and to a lesser degree on the nineteenth- and twentieth-century South in the form of "Baptist" blue laws.

What of the new Southern Baptist President? Has he brought to the Oval Office secret schemes to bring in a new kind of prohibition based upon "shortages" and austerity drives? Will he propose bizarre programs to save the institution of marriage by stiffening the divorce laws? Will he organize or lend his name to a crusade against what puritans everywhere agree is the plague of pornography? Will he demand that America be pure of mind and body as well as of heart?

Probably not. Carter is himself a moderate person, personally pure and upright despite a few lapses in language now and then, but he is a rather typical Southern Baptist: less puritan than his church's official policies. He is also a pragmatic politician. He knows, as he has shown in his limited exercise of power as governor of Georgia, that this is a pluralist society. He might, in armchair conversations, toy with some seemingly old-fashioned prescriptions for American society's ills; but he is too smart to try to impose his personal standards on the population at large.

He might, on the other hand, translate some of his early puritan training into stricter codes of governmental accountability. He has already begun to demand higher standards of integrity of the executive branch and encourage the same in the legislative branch. In the decade following so much graft and corruption in all levels of government, when politicians are rated just ahead of used-car dealers in public respect, this kind of Baptist puritanism might not be such a bad thing.

2. Southern Baptists are theists. They believe in a God who is a real Being. They believe that God acts in history and in the lives of individuals. They believe that God calls every person to salvation. They believe that he leads the receptive heart to know what to do in every crisis of life. They believe that he is the authority in every Christian's life. They believe, after the Biblical injunction, that they should obey God rather than man.

Jimmy Carter is known in this area of Baptist theology to be more than orthodox. He prays daily and sometimes hourly. He reads his New Testament every night. He claims to ask God for direction. This can be both comforting and alarming to concerned citizens. It might mean that in true Protestant-Baptist fashion he will follow no advice that contradicts what he believes before God is right. It might also mean that he will at crucial times reject the advice, or perhaps not even listen to the advice, of reasonable men and women.

Carter is known to be a loner. Fellow students, buddies on naval assignments, colleagues in the Georgia senate, acquaintances and employees during his years as governor and on the Presidential campaign trail all universally agree that personally he is distant, a man very much to himself—brilliant, able, pragmatic, honest, but very much alone. Can such a man who does not often ask advice of others, who believes in a God who speaks directly to him without mitigating media, be trusted with the "most perilous decisions" of the "most powerful office in the world" today? Is there a chance a theist like this might, as some have warned, take his initials J.C. too seriously? Is there danger of a "messianic" Presidency?

The Presidency today can indeed be a dangerous office for a man without his feet firmly planted on earth. With high-ranking officials jumping to grant every wish, with the power to affect the lives of every person on the planet, the "man behind the seal" can very easily come to believe in his own omnipotence and omniscience. This delusion is what helped destroy the promising Johnson and Nixon Presidencies. It is a danger for any man. Will it be more a danger for a born-again Southern Baptist whose personality is by his own admission a mixture of Georgia mud turtle and mystic?

Probably not. Carter's feet are pretty firmly planted. His noted mysticism is greatly exaggerated. He prays and seeks divine guidance, yes, but he has never been known to follow such guidance when it contradicted good political reason. His seems to be the type of mind that Southern Baptists jokingly call "English walnut." He actually keeps his religion and his politics, the mystical and the practical, in separate compartments. The mud turtle might be dangerous; the mystic is not.

3. Southern Baptists are evangelistic. They have been saved by grace. They believe that it is their duty to share the good news of their salvation with others. Mission- and revival-minded, they feel it their duty to witness around the world. They are a wonder to watch. My own father, a Presbyterian married to a Southern Baptist, once told me he simply hadn't the physical stamina to join my mother's church. Will Rogers once wrote that the government builds roads so Baptists can wear them out going to and from revival meetings.

On this point Jimmy Carter is a very good Southern Baptist. He has served as a lay missionary to Massachusetts. He has served on the Southern Baptist Brotherhood Commission, an organization that encourages Southern Baptist men to support world missions. In his autobiography, *Why Not the Best?* he confesses his failure to be a good Christian by comparing the millions of hands he shook running for office to the hundreds he shook witnessing for the Lord in a particular year.

Will this evangelistic Southern Baptist President try to be some sort of political missionary? Will he bring from his Baptist Young People's Union missionary training a zeal to win "the lost" around the world? Will he come to believe that American values and institutions, like Christian salvation, are needed everywhere? Will he, encouraged by American business interests, equate "our side" with the forces of good and "theirs" with evil? Will he try to save our little "red and yellow, black and white" brothers around the globe from a fate worse than death?

Eric Goldman in *The Tragedy of Lyndon Johnson* blamed southern Protestantism's missionary mind for L.B.J.'s decision to "save" Vietnam. Goldman said L.B.J.'s image of an Asia waiting to be converted to Western life, an image created by the slide lectures of returning missionaries, made his mistake inevitable. Would Jimmy Carter the lay missionary make a similar mistake? Would there be other Vietnams?

There might be. But such dangers are no more likely under Jimmy Carter than under any other male his age. Carter, who has lived more than half his life since 1945, who has along with the nation been tempered by what we all hope have been the "lessons" of Vietnam, is as trustworthy as anyone else.

Again, Carter is pragmatic. He knows he cannot involve America in new wars without overwhelming opposition from both Congress and the people. His choice of the quiet but capable Cyrus Vance for Secretary of State seems an indication of his determination to work for peace and not conflict in a pluralist world. The greatest threat of conflict lies probably not in Jimmy Carter's religious mind but in the Democrats' fear of being called soft on Communism.

Carter, a fiscal conservative, a disciple of free enterprise, will most likely support overseas investments of American business. Carter the missionary will probably strengthen the Peace Corps. The only danger his evangelistic training might cause would be his expectation of quick results and rapid change. Whether the Georgian with the relatively limited foreign experience can adjust to the agonizing snail's pace of diplomacy remains to be seen. To fear that he might interpret modern history through apocalyptic visions is unmerited.

4. Southern Baptists also are, as their critics readily point out, an isolated people. Theologically and ecclesiastically they keep to themselves. They might occasionally join other denominations for community Easter, Thanksgiving, Christmas, and revival services, but these times are rare. This self-imposed estrangement is due in part to their fundamentalism. But fundamentalism has led some conservative churches to form ties with other fundamentalist groups, drawing together as true brothers against the secular world and liberal churches, forming anti-ecumenical ecumenical fundamentalist organizations.

Southern Baptists, however, feel superior to other fundamentalist groups. The landmarkist movement, using softer voices and words, is still very much alive among them. They know in their bones that they are the True Church, reaching back across an unbroken trail of blood to the apostles, and they see no good reason to contaminate or dilute their precious heritage by association with lesser churches.

All of this has left Jimmy Carter, as various religious spokesmen have noticed, with little knowledge of other Christian and non-Christian denominations. He is theologically and ecclesiastically parochial, more so perhaps than most American Presidents have been. He is a Southern Baptist. As President he attends a Washington Baptist church. He will not try to fuzz his affiliation as other Presidents have. He will have no White House Sunday services with a different brand of minister each week. But this does not mean he will be intolerant of other groups. His early years outside the South, his four years as governor of "all" Georgians, his two years of running for President have broadened his understanding of religious variety. During the campaign he told a predominantly Jewish audience:

> I worship the same God you do; we [Baptists] study the same Bible you do. This is a country wherein one's own religious faith should not be a matter of prejudice or concern. The ability of Jews, Catholics, Baptists, even atheists to work in harmony with one another in our nation, based on a system of religious pluralism, is one that is precious to me.

Such things are expected from political candidates. Even Richard Nixon, said by intimates to be personally anti-Semitic, would not have argued with this Carter vision. We can hope he is sincere. A Southern Baptist, liberated from regional and denominational prejudices the way Carter appears to be, might well be good for the country's religions. He would uphold religious freedom. He would oppose federal aid to religious institutions.

He would support the recent Supreme Court ban on public school prayer. He might well receive his greatest criticism from the very people who taught him all these things and then forgot them: the Southern Baptists.

5. Southern Baptists are also democrats. From earliest beginnings they have given rule to the people and popular majority. Even the encroachments of denominationalism that seeks to make local churches conform and a fundamentalism that seeks to make individuals in local churches conform have not been able to erase the deep imprint of this democracy. Despite modern stress and strain, the people still rule. The pastor is their servant.

Jimmy Carter has learned this Baptist lesson well. He says in his autobiography that from Leo Tolstoy's *War and Peace,* a book he read as a child and has reread many times since, a book he says helped mold his philosophy of life, he learned that "the course of human events—even the greatest historical events—is determined ultimately not by the leaders but by the common, ordinary people. Their hopes and dreams, their doubts and fears, their courage and tenacity, their quiet commitments determine the destiny of the world." Such eloquent words from a nuts-and-bolts politician not known for his elevated speech is probably significant. Jimmy Carter waxes eloquent not over sunrises or river mist or even summit conferences, only over "the people."

In his acceptance speech at the Democratic National Convention he said, "It is time for the people to run the government, and not the other way around." He continued, "The tragedy of Vietnam and Cambodia, the disgrace of Watergate, and the embarrassment of the CIA revelations could have been avoided if our government had reflected the sound judgment, good common sense, and high moral character of the American people." He also said, "Our nation should always derive its character directly from our people and let this be the strength and the image to be presented to the world."

Carter's belief in the right of a "good" people to run its own affairs translates for Carter into a demand that government be conducted in the open. He told Bill Moyers in his interview that the most obvious and important lesson of the last decade is that the President should "strip away secrecy of government" and open up the deliberations of the executive and legislative branches. He said he would "like to see Cabinet members go before joint sessions of Congress to be examined and questioned." Presumably he will hold regular press conferences as he has promised, and tell the truth about every position he takes.

No one can say, however, whether he will in fact be a true democrat. The pressures of diplomacy and vested interests, the realization that to get to the people he must go through a sometimes unsympathetic press with a tendency to interpret every word, may make him conclude that his early enthusiasm for openness, for sharing knowledge and power with a decent people who have the right to know what their leaders are doing and who will make the right decision if given all the facts, was a bit naive. But we must say he seems headed in the right direction. It is also a Baptist direction.

"You need to have an open government," Carter has said. "You need to tell the truth. A minimum of secrecy. Let the people have a maximum part to play in the evolution and consummation of our domestic and foreign policies." In the past when a politician spoke of "the people," a person was wise to speak up and ask him, which people? The aristocracy? The bourgeoisie? The proletariat? The young, the old, the union, the country club? For Carter it is, by his own words, *all* the people, especially those who are in need, those without a voice, those who can't help themselves, but *all.*

6. Southern Baptists are people of the Book. Theirs is a Biblical faith. Though they are sometimes a bit inconsistent about which parts they accept and apply, though they have their own peculiar interpretations of certain passages, they claim and to a large extent have the right to the title. The Bible is to some Southern Baptists almost an idol, a paper pope as it has been said. One of their churches near Cincinnati, Ohio, boasts a pulpit perched atop a giant replica of an Oxford edition King James Version red-letter edition New Testament. Things often get out of hand this way. But the message of this Bible they so cherish, if it is not obscured by imposed interpretations, is one of love and peace—not a bad message for a President to

cherish. It teaches that God loves his created order and literally became a man to share human community. It makes sacred the world and its people. It calls upon leaders to serve them well. Again, not bad.

Carter reads his New Testament—in Spanish—every night. He seems by most indications to understand what he reads. He appears able to separate all the various interpretations, even the Baptist ones, from the simple meanings of the text. Had he "felt the call," he might have made a good expository preacher or perhaps even a professor of theology. His espousal of "the whole gospel" has at times caused him to make some rather unusual political statements, such as the time he promised to support Israel's independence and territorial integrity because the Bible says God intends the Jews to have a place to live. Quite often he has made theologically insightful comments, especially in the *Playboy* interview. He has demonstrated a good amount of Biblical insight.

Take, for example, his doctrine of forgiveness as applied to draft evaders. On August 29, 1976, at a time when false steps were disastrous, Carter unveiled to an American Legion Convention in Seattle his program to recover this group of young Americans. Deserters would be treated on a case by case basis, he said; but to draft evaders, those who for various reasons chose to leave the country rather than be drafted, he would grant an unconditional pardon. He would not grant amnesty, which would mean that what the young men had done was right;

he would give them pardon, which meant that right or wrong they were forgiven.

In 1974, Gerald Ford had issued an order of clemency to an estimated 14,000 of the 113,000 Vietnam war exiles. They could return home in exchange for certain public service compensatory work. They had a year to decide. Some critics said he did this only to offset the adverse effects of pardoning Richard Nixon. Many theologians, despite sympathy for Nixon in his bad health, found fault with Ford on both counts. He would force the young men to earn their salvation by works. He would hand Nixon cheap grace.

On his first full day as President, Carter invited all the draft evaders home, without time limits, without works. This is Biblical grace. It does demand implicit confession of guilt. To accept pardon is to admit sin. (Thus Leon Jaworski said of Nixon as well.) But it also offers love and forgiveness regardless of original intent. Perhaps this is not perfect Biblical doctrine, but it is close. Again, the very people who taught Carter to look in the Bible for his faith will probably criticize him the most for this act of pardon.

7. Finally, Southern Baptists are salvationists. They believe not so much in original sin as in the native estrangement of the individual from God. Every child is destined (find one who doesn't) to sin. Each person's soul is his own responsibility.

God in Christ through the Holy Spirit—usually

working through human media—comes to every person with the gift of salvation. It is free, without strings, a grace. Each person has the free will to accept or reject it. When accepted, it changes one's life. One is still imperfect, still bound by many of the same sinful desires, still prone to stumble, but now desires heaven and earthly holiness. Renewal of vows made as a result but not as a condition of salvation usually happens many times, but salvation is once for all.

Southern Baptists have had to work rather hard to correct certain perversions of their doctrine of salvation. One is the tendency of salvation to turn the Christian's mind toward preoccupation with spiritual experience and away from acts of social concern that should flow from gratitude to God for salvation. Another is the tendency to consider this life only a training ground for the next and to remain pure and untouched by association with this world. Salvation can make one selfish.

Jimmy Carter is perhaps the perfect specimen of the saved Southern Baptist. His salvation has given him inner peace, security, and assurance. It has not turned him from his responsibility to the here and now. According to his own confession, it has made him love others as he is loved by God. He says it has released a flow of love for his fellowman. This is the kind of salvation that enlightened Southern Baptist ministers have preached for generations. It is responsible for most of the good that Southern Baptists have done in the world.

Both Jimmy Carter and his Southern Baptist faith will continue to be on trial during the remaining years of his Presidency. The world of religion will carefully examine his record to answer the following questions:

1. Did he really learn from his faith? How effective is religious education among the Southern Baptists? How well does its theology penetrate the walls of social and personal prejudice?

2. What did it teach him? Did it teach him the true New Testament message or local, regional, national interpretations?

3. How do the teachings of Southern Baptists—and, in a more general sense, of Christians as a whole—work in the practical task of redeeming the times?

In time we will know. The Baptist faith, warts and all, has a grand tradition. A number of its teachings seem appropriate for a President's philosophy of life. Now we will see for sure.

Chapter V

The Secular City:
Politics as Ministry

THE TWENTIETH CENTURY, with all its hopes and despairs, its tragedies and triumphs, has profoundly affected the American church and altered American religious thought. The two world wars, the Great Depression, and the strange new world of atomic diplomacy have each in turn touched and reshaped our institutions and our values. Each decade, it seems, has in its own way erased and rewritten sections of our credo.

This was true of the '60s, the decade of J.F.K. and L.B.J., of Martin Luther King and the Vietnam war, the decade in which Jimmy Carter came to political maturity. This was the decade in which ever more churchmen left the safety of their stained-glass shadows to march down littered streets in behalf of social justice. It was the time when more and more Christian leaders at last came to see, with Walter Rauschenbusch of the 1890's and Reinhold Niebuhr of the 1930's, that the true servant of God works to make life here and now better for those he is trying to save.

One of the most popular "religious" books of the

'60s was *The Secular City*, by Harvey Cox. Cox captured the spirit of the movement already under way and gave it a poetic voice. He argued, and thousands of clergymen and laymen agreed, that God calls his people not to run away and hide from the world but calls them into the world, the secular city, the city of man, into the institutions of society, to redeem them, to fight oppression and despair, to save people for earth as well as for heaven.

With the end of the '60s, with Richard Nixon firmly in control, with campus unrest silenced by guns and an economic recession that threatened the security of social offenders, with the war in Vietnam growing old and tiresome if not less deadly, things seemed to change, and religion with them. An odd, uneasy quiet settled. The younger religious generation seemed suddenly preoccupied with their own souls, with personal salvation, even with prayer again. Some of the dropouts of the '60s, older and still without much hope, rediscovered the fundamentalism of their youth and except for hair and beads became very much like their parents. A new decade, and with it a new religious time, had begun.

Yet just as the effects of earlier decades had not fully disappeared, as they lived on in certain permanent flavors and styles, so the effects of the '60s were not really dead. Their more phenomenal eruptions were indeed gone, but not the abiding commitment to racial equality, social justice, and economic opportunity. Today even the most rigid of fundamentalists will acknowledge the place of Christian social work. A new "underground" troop of radical Biblicists, once protest marchers, are abroad in the land advocating a total commitment to the Christ of the Bible and his plan for social as well as spiritual revolution. The '60s live on.

Jimmy Carter, thirty-six years old when John Kennedy was elected President, a Southern Baptist living in Sumter County, Georgia, was not too far off the main highway to miss the effects of the frightening decade ahead. During that decade he ran successfully for state senator and first unsuccessfully and then again successfully for governor of Georgia. He had long been taught by his church that every Christian, regardless of profession, must help take the good news to a needy world. He had been taught, in good Southern Baptist tradition, that every believer is a priest, granted by God the right and power and duty to minister to the needs of those inside and outside the church. The 1960's and their prophetic voices taught him that the needs of the world are not merely spiritual (at least they are not filled merely by prayer and witness) and that the good news (of earth as well as heaven) can be preached, that the Christian can minister to the world through a profession many Southern Baptists considered irredeemable, elective politics.

In his autobiography Carter tells of a conversation with a minister who visited Plains in 1962, the year Carter decided to run for the state senate. They were discussing ways to serve the public interest, a discussion doubtless initiated by Carter, when he told the minister he was thinking of running for office. "The pastor was surprised that I would consider going into politics," Carter says, "and strongly advised me not to become involved in such a discredited profession. We had a rather heated argument, and he finally asked, 'If you want to be of service to other people, why don't you go into the ministry or into some honorable social service work?' On the spur of the moment I retorted, 'How would you like to be pastor of a church with 80,000 members?' He finally admitted that it was possible to stay honest and at the same time minister to the needs of the 80,000 citizens of the 14th senate district." Although his first race for governor and his subsequent experience of despair and renewal or "rebirth" were still four years away, Carter was already a deacon and a thoughtful Christian. He knew Baptist traditions. He knew what was happening in his world. He had already begun to think of politics as ministry.

This is not to say his motives in running for office were exclusively altruistic. Politicians want recognition and power. So did, so does Jimmy Carter. But one can be motivated by two or more desires at once. It seems probable that Carter has all along been guided by a desire to succeed to power and once in office to minister to the needs of those who gave him the power to do good.

Carter's concept of ministry, though many of his brethren—like the minister in Plains—would fail to recognize it as their own, is essentially Southern Baptist. It was expanded by his personal experiences and by the social movements of American religion in the '60s. It has been further enlarged and enlightened by the books Carter has read.

Carter, unlike our last several Presidents, loves to read. He remembers fondly the day electricity came to his home and the "glorious" light let him read far into every night. Through the years he has traveled with books, using every spare moment to read. His fellow officers at sea recall how at night when they played cards he would curl up with a stack of instruction manuals. Political friends recall his enthusiasm for books on politics and religion and how the two relate. Among the authors whom Carter remembers as having had more than passing influence on him are Leo Tolstoy, Charles Darwin, Bertrand Russell, James Agee, William Faulkner, Paul Tillich, and Reinhold Niebuhr, all of whom share a common interest in religion as an integral part of the lives of people struggling for freedom and dignity.

Tillich and Niebuhr, not the usual fare for Southern Baptist laymen, especially politicians, are interesting choices. It is doubtful that Carter really understands either man in a comprehensive or systematic way. Yet the passages from their writings that he enjoys quoting usually capture the central theme of the book from which they are taken, indicating that Carter does understand what he has read.

Paul Tillich, a German Lutheran theologian, was the first Christian professor expelled by Hitler and the Nazis after their victory in 1933. He came to live and work in the United States at the invitation of American theologians who saw his accomplishments and potential, and he spent the second half of his long and distinguished career at Union Theological Seminary in Manhattan, at Harvard University, and at the Divinity School of the University of Chicago.

Perhaps Tillich's greatest contribution to modern theology was his effort to express the Christian message in the terminology of twentieth-century philosophy, especially that philosophy which seemed most authentically to be speaking for the feelings of twentieth-century man, existentialism. For Tillich, a missionary, a minister to secular society, God was not so much some Great Person as he was the Ground of Being. God neither was nor was not—he was both "is" and "is not." He held within himself all things, good and evil, maleness and femaleness, dark and light, life and death. Christ, for Tillich, was the New Being. Faith was Ultimate Concern which leads to the great quest for the Ground of Being. The person who participates in Ultimate Concern is part of the New Being. Tillich, confusing to the uninitiated, inspiring to the thoughtful, provides one of the most interesting and creative of the various responses to the dilemma of modern secular society.

Carter, when he spoke with Bill Moyers, quoted Tillich to the effect that "religion is a search for the relationship between us and God and us and our fellow human beings." When we quit searching for these relationships, Carter went on to explain, we have lost our religion. This is essential Tillich—and essential Carter. Religious faith is the great quest,

96

the quest for God, yes, but also for other human beings. Carter went on to interpret: "When we become self-satisfied, proud, sure, at that point we lose the self-searching, the humility, the subservience to God's will, the more intimate understanding of other people's needs, the more inclination to be accommodating, and, in that instant, we lose our religion."

Carter is of course not as concise or profound as Tillich, but it is obvious the two agree. For Carter, following Tillich the Christian Socialist, concern for the needs of people (Carter's congregation numbers 212,000,000 now) is religion. Politics as ministry. Tillich would have been proud of his disciple in Washington.

Carter also speaks often of Reinhold Niebuhr. Niebuhr, in fact, is his favorite religious writer. This seems a bit odd when one recalls that only a few years ago Niebuhr was said by many Southern Baptist preachers to be an enemy of all things American and Christian.

Niebuhr was born in Missouri in 1892 and from 1915 to 1928 was pastor of an inner-city church in Detroit. There he confronted face-to-face the injustices of America's celebrated industrial revolution and slowly made a name for himself faulting the humanitarianism of Henry Ford. His writings earned him a position on the faculty of Union Theological Seminary in New York City in 1928, and from there he helped transform America's liberal theological tradition. Believed by many to be the most original philosophical mind of the past two hundred years, he combined a somewhat conservative theology with a radical social reform spirit to produce one of the most convincing arguments for Christian Socialism ever heard.

It was in the early '60s, about the time Carter was choosing politics as a career, that William Gunther, now an associate justice of the Georgia supreme court, gave Carter his first Niebuhr book. Entitled *Reinhold Niebuhr on Politics,* it was a systematized collection of articles, essays, and excerpts from Niebuhr's long religiopolitical career. Niebuhr spoke directly to Carter. He commended simple acts of kindness on the personal Christian level, but he warned that love on a grander scale must be applied differently. For someone in politics, "love" must be translated "justice."

He also said that the man who wanted to establish love-justice in his society must have power. In *Moral Man and Immoral Society* he explained that it is possible to establish justice between individuals through "moral and rational suasion" but that the relationship between social and economic groups is "political" rather than "ethical" and "will be determined by the proportion of power which each group possesses at least as much as by any rational and moral appraisal of the comparative needs and claims of each group." Thus the man who wants to show love for and establish love among his fellowmen (Carter's congregation of 212,000,000) must have the power and the position to establish justice. "The sad duty of politics," Carter so often quotes Niebuhr, "is to establish justice in a sinful world."

To establish justice one must have power. Power must be in the hands of a good man, or it will be used to establish or perpetuate injustice. Good men must run for office. They must use power in a godly manner to teach and establish love-justice. They must be ministers.

In *Courage to Change,* another Niebuhr book that Carter has read and quoted, Niebuhr said, "In the process of building communities every impulse of love must be translated into simple justice." In *The Children of Light and the Children of Darkness,* he said, "Man's capacity for justice makes democracy possible; but man's inclination to injustice makes democracy necessary." Carter has obviously made such statements part of his philosophy. In his acceptance speech at the Democratic National Convention, he borrowed Niebuhr's exact words: "Love must be aggressively translated into simple justice." And he told Bill Moyers that his first responsibility as a political leader is "to try to establish justice." He was speaking of Christian love.

Considering his religious and intellectual orientation, his Baptist missionary spirit, his Niebuhrian social ethics, his political baptism of fire in the '60s, it should not have been so surprising to hear that "Reverend" Carter, soon after his nomination for President, had granted an interview to *Playboy* magazine. But quite a number of his earlier supporters, many Southern Baptists, many who had admired his earlier "ministerial" image, were downright shocked. Almost every church spokesman interviewed at the time, from every degree of the political and theological spectrum, agreed that Carter was hurt by the flap that followed. No one thought it helped him. A Roper poll at the end of the campaign showed that it had little final influence on the way most Americans voted, but at the time, through most of September, it caused among puritans some kind of old-fashioned uproar.

Carter had appeared between the covers (sheets?) of a pornographic magazine. *Playboy* was not considered quite so bad, by current standards, as it had been back when it was all alone in its field; but Hugh Hefner's scandalous service to prurient interests was certainly no place for a Presidential candidate, especially a born-again Christian, to show his wares. It was even reported, though few knew firsthand for two weeks and more, that he had used two shady euphemisms.

In point of fact, Jimmy Carter did not himself make the appointment with *Playboy* interviewers. This was done by his press secretary, Jody Powell. But Carter agreed voluntarily to meet the commitment. Some people said he did it to help shed his ministerial image, but a careful reading indicates that this was not the case. He obviously thought such an interview would give him needed publicity, and he didn't count on the conservative reaction to it, but there is every reason to believe that he actually wanted to reach the *Playboy* audience. It may have been a mistake. It may have demonstrated an unforgivable naiveté to think the *Playboy* audience would want to know how he felt about domestic and international affairs and his religious faith, but it is hard to fault his desire to be a minister.

All of Carter's headaches with the interview grew out of the last of the several conversations he permitted, just as the *Playboy* editor was leaving. The editor asked one final question, whether Carter thought giving such an interview would hurt him, and Carter launched into a long final statement. It was personal and emotional. Someone showed him that the *Playboy* tape was still running, but he brushed the warning aside and went on. What he said was sheer poetry. He explained what Baptists believe. He gave a sermon on hypocrisy. Finally, having been asked over and over during the past two days about sexual ethics, he let go.

He explained that he tried not to sin, but he admitted that Christ's standards are very high. Christ, he reminded the editor, said that anyone who looks at a woman with lust sins. He had looked on a lot of women with lust. He had sinned in his heart many times. God always forgave him. So he couldn't very well condemn someone who leaves his wife and "shacks up" with another woman. Christ also warned against judging others. "Christ says, don't consider yourself better than someone else because one guy screws a whole bunch of women while the other guy is loyal to his wife." Then came the promise not to lie and cheat the American people, as Johnson and Nixon had done.

This was the only passage of the entire interview —about 3 percent of it—to get national coverage. The news media, looking as usual for the spectacular, talked of Carter's lust and adultery. Not only did reporters overlook most of what he said, they overlooked why he said it as well.

The week the snippets were released and spread abroad, still two weeks before the average churchman could buy this issue of *Playboy* on the stands, Southern Baptists and other conservative evangelicals began a painful, soul-searching reappraisal of the Carter candidacy. Not even his liberalism on race and on the economy had bothered them so much. Why would the man they trusted do such a thing? Was he really what they had thought he was? Should they in fact vote Democratic against their economic and racial interests if Carter associated with such people and used such language? Carter's pastor in Plains was so distressed by the controversy in his own denomination that he released an open letter to Southern Baptists. As printed in Baptist papers in Georgia, it read: "After reading the interview with *Playboy,* I am afraid that I must accept the responsibility for his accepting the interview. I have been his pastor for two years and have always taught all my people to take advantage of every opportunity to share our faith in Christ."

This is what the pastor felt Carter had tried to do. It is doubtless what Carter himself thought he was doing. It was interesting to see how few evangelicals understood his motives and recognized the apt interpretation and application of Christ's teachings on purity of heart and the lust of the mind, not to mention forgiveness and the warning not to judge others lest you yourself be judged.

Southern Baptist reaction to the interview was of course mixed. Wally Amos Criswell, longtime pastor of the First Baptist Church of Dallas, past president of the Southern Baptist Convention, a leader of the conservative but still loyal wing of Southern Baptists, decided it was time for him to follow his economic inclinations. Gerald Ford, in Dallas to see the Oklahoma-Texas football game, attended services at the First Baptist Church. There Criswell denounced *Playboy* as "pornographic" and "salacious" and commended Ford for allegedly refusing them an interview. The congregation applauded. On the front steps at the close of the service, he endorsed Ford for President and said that while he was glad Carter was born again, he just didn't like his politics.

On the other hand, a somewhat younger Texas Southern Baptist, Buckner Fanning of San Antonio, spoke that same weekend (October 9–10) at the Texas Baptist Student Convention in Houston. He commended Carter for doing the interview in *Playboy.* He compared it to Billy Graham's appearances on Johnny Carson's *Tonight* show. Christians, he said, should take their message out into the world. His audience of younger Texas Baptists applauded. In Bob Dylan's words, the times they are achangin'.

The president of the Southern Baptist Convention, James Sullivan, retired head of the Baptist Sunday School Board, also commended Carter for his efforts to minister to the *Playboy* people. He waited, however, until after the election, when Carter was safely elected with 60 percent of the Southern Baptist vote.

The *Playboy* interview had been for quite a number of Southern Baptists the one most important event of the Presidential campaign. Lutheran church historian Martin Marty of *The Christian Century* was one of the few religious commentators of any denomination to see the humor in the whole crazy episode. He gave Carter warm regards but low marks for trying to minister this way. He said he had tried it himself and it didn't work. First, it was only conservative churchmen, puritans, who read such interviews—and they only to criticize. Second, the typical *Playboy* reader, the swinger, was so Biblically illiterate he probably thought, if he thought at all, that Carter was making up the Sermon on the Mount's admonition that lust is in the mind. Third, Carter chose the wrong example. Instead of saying he had lusted in his mind and was therefore an adulterer, he should have said he had been angry with a brother and was therefore a murderer. Most people could more easily vote for a murderer than for an adulterer.

Most Southern Baptists, most conservative evangelicals, whether for or against Carter's attempt to minister, found no such humor in the interview.

The Southern Baptist attitude toward their most famous political figure, the man who has most successfully taken his message of faith into the secular city, is at best mixed. During the late spring and early summer, after Carter had won the primaries and after Southern Baptists had learned of his faith and affiliation, after he was seen to be "one of us" who might be President, he was "the one" for Southern Baptists. Poor Gerald Ford came to speak at the Southern Baptist Convention which was meeting in Norfolk, Virginia, and raised his biggest cheer when he mentioned Carter's name. Carter's book sold out that same day. Brother Bailey Smith of the First Southern Baptist Church of Del City, Oklahoma, told the delegates that it was time for America to have a born-again President. It would be improper to give his name at the Convention, he mused, but his initials were "the same as our Lord's." No one had to ask which candidate was meant.

Southern Baptists had not come so close to taking an open stand on a Presidential contest since 1960 when as many Southern Baptist preachers warned anguished congregations against voting for the attractive but Catholic Kennedy as there were nuns to turn out to assure his election. I remember attending a conference that summer at the Southern Baptist New Mexico retreat called Glorieta. I was told I shouldn't vote for a man who got his money from whiskey, his religion from Rome, and his haircut from a five-year-old boy. It was the closest I have ever come to walking out on a religious service.

The pro-Carter sentiment, at least as a visible, publicized phenomenon among Southern Baptists, was short-lived. He never lost his Southern Baptist lead, but the enthusiasm declined with the percentage. This was in part due to Gerald Ford's ever-increasing piosity, in part to the *Playboy* interview, and in part to the gradual realization that Carter was a real Democrat; but it was perhaps due mostly to Carter's willingness to meet the secular world on its own turf and terms, to appeal to its votes and offer it in return a taste of his faith, to live in Tillich's phrase on the borderlines of life. Southern Baptists, puritan, isolated from the world out there, grew less and less to recognize their own product.

One prominent Southern Baptist caught in the middle of the campaign was Evangelist Billy Graham. Raised a Presbyterian, educated in independent evangelical schools, Graham has been a Southern Baptist with membership in the First Baptist Church of Dallas since he burst on the national scene a quarter century ago. He has generally leaned toward Republican candidates, especially in Presidential elections, and in 1968 he broke his traditional "neutral stance so I can work with any President" to support Richard Nixon. Nixon had appeared at Graham's meeting in New York City in 1957. Now in 1968, Graham permitted himself to be filmed in Nixon's audiences, a tacit show of support. Even after Nixon was forced to resign, Graham found fault with him only for the bad language on the tapes, and he made it clear that he considered the revelations about Kennedy's women as bad as those about Nixon's obstruction of justice.

In 1976 a fellow Southern Baptist, a man who said openly he considered Jesus the most important thing in his life, a born-again believer who brought his religious faith to politics and now wanted to be President, was the Democratic candidate. Could Graham, who has called for such men to step forward for years, afford to support him? Could he afford not to? He was at last freed from having to decide by Ford's claim that he too was saved, but in September he did say, "I would rather have a man in office who is highly qualified to be President who didn't make much of a religious profession than to have a man who had no qualifications but who made a religious profession." He said no more. He did drop by to visit Gerald Ford at the White House the week the *Playboy* flap erupted.

Carter won. He was not Graham's friend. Graham suddenly began boasting of America's capacity to elect a born-again, Bible-carrying Baptist President, but it was probably too late. Unless he is able to work his way back into Carter's good graces, he may prove to be one of the losers in 1976.

Graham's dilemma was caused by his need for financial backing from the rich, conservative businessmen who are so often found supporting religion that keeps the workingman in his place. His crusades have always been heavily underwritten by the Pews and the Jarmans and the members of Criswell's conservative congregation, all of whom feel their interests are best served by Republicans. Perhaps Graham has come to feel that way too. Perhaps, as David Frye teases him, he has indeed come to enjoy $300 suits more than sackcloth.

Perhaps Graham's problem is the whole church's problem. Alliances to raise money for missions sometimes take away the true meaning and purpose and scope and manner of the mission. Jimmy Carter seems to have hurdled this problem.

Jimmy Carter, a politician who sees politics as a means of ministry, is President. Keep watching for him to use the highest office in the land to bring the good news to the secular city. He might do this in several ways:

1. The Presidency, as Teddy Roosevelt used to say, is a bully pulpit. It is the perfect place to exhort and instruct the American people in the ways of love-justice.

2. It is also the best place from which to set a high moral tone of decency and honesty.

3. It is a place of power from which to help the oppressed, from which a man can translate love into simple justice.

4. It is the best place to teach the democracy that man's capacity for injustice makes necessary. Carter might well be able, by drawing from his Baptist and Democratic backgrounds, by being not an elected king but simply first among equals, to teach this lesson well.

Part of Carter's ministry will be to preach. Preaching has in recent years lost some of its respect. To preach has come to mean to bore people with meaningless rhetoric. But preaching, if done well and wisely, is one of the Christian messenger's greatest tools. Perhaps Carter's sermons might follow the pattern he set down in, of all places, his *Playboy* interview. There he said:

108

What Christ taught about most was pride, that one person should never think he was any better than anybody else. One of the most vivid stories Christ told in one of his parables was about two people who went into a church. One was an official of the church, a Pharisee, and he said, "Lord, I thank you that I'm not like all those other people. I keep all your commandments, I give a tenth of everything I own. I'm here to give thanks for making me more acceptable in your sight." The other guy was despised by the nation, and he went in, prostrated himself on the floor and said, "Lord, have mercy on me, a sinner. I'm not worthy to lift my eyes to heaven." Christ asked the disciples which of the two had justified his life. The answer was obviously the one who was humble.

It would be hard to find a better sermon for a President of the United States to preach to us and listen to himself.

Perhaps to conclude such a sermon Carter might use the following prayer written by Reinhold Niebuhr in 1934. Niebuhr gave the prayer away to a member of the congregation the day it was delivered, and the man had it published. It later became the watch-prayer for Alcoholics Anonymous. It might well serve President Carter:

> O God:
> Give us serenity to accept what cannot
> be changed, courage to change what
> should be changed, and wisdom
> to distinguish the one from
> the other.
> Amen.

Chapter VI

A New Tune out of Dixie:
The Family Snopes and Jimmy Carter

ON SUNDAY MORNING, October 31, 1976, two days before Americans were to choose a new President, a small convoy of out-of-town cars pulled up and stopped near the Plains Baptist Church, Sumter County, Georgia. In recent months the local residents had grown accustomed to strangers in their town, first a trickle and then a shower of them, but they knew that this group was different. They had been warned. They were ready.

The leader of the convoy stepped out and walked to the front steps of the church. He was a dapper man for his considerable size. His suit was well-tailored. He wore a white shirt with a black stripe around the clerical collar and down the front. His hair was close-cropped and graying. He was a Negro. His name was Clennon King. He was a preacher from nearby Albany. He had come to integrate Plains Baptist.

At the front steps he met the pastor of the church, the Reverend Bruce Edwards, a simple man who over the past six months had found himself under

110

tremendous unexpected pressures. Clennon King told him he had come to attend church. Mr. Edwards announced to him that his deacons had voted earlier in the week to cancel today's services. Mr. King said he would return the following Sunday. They both knew that the services had been canceled because Mr. King had made public his intention to come and join the all-white Southern Baptist church.

Clennon King, new to most Americans who watched or read about this bizarre scene—a church closing its doors rather than admit a black man in 1976—was an old, experienced hand at public spectacle and rejection. He had been the first black to try to enroll at the University of Mississippi, four years before James Meredith successfully did so. He had been carried out and held incommunicado for twenty hours before being confined to a mental institution for over a week. He had also been found guilty of "breaking and entering" a church where he was no longer pastor and he had served time for nonsupport of his family.

Many people said the attempt to integrate Plains Baptist Church was a Republican trick to hurt Jimmy Carter. King said he came because God had told him to be there. He had read an extract from one of Mr. Edwards' sermons saying that all people should be welcomed into God's house. He let the church know he was coming. The deacons said no. Mr. Edwards relayed their decision to the public and said that he did not agree. The deacons said that Mr. Edwards was acting too independently, that all the publicity had gone to his head, and they voted to fire him.

The Baptist church in Plains had been founded in 1836. For the first half century of its life as Lebanon Baptist Church, it had served both black and white members. Before the turn of the century, following a pattern all over the South, the races were divided and two churches emerged, one black and one white. Blacks occasionally visited Plains Baptist and whites occasionally visited Lebanon Baptist, the blacks having kept the original name. In 1965, when blacks were knocking on hundreds of doors of schools and churches Plains Baptist, with only Jimmy Carter's immediate family objecting, voted to refuse admittance to blacks or other troublemakers. This was of course the right of any Southern Baptist church. Many churches in the Deep South did the same thing at this time.

The Reverend Clennon King returned to Plains Baptist on November 7. Again the doors were locked. Again there was no service.

On November 14, instead of the regular morning service, a business meeting was held—for church members only. The Presidential election was over. Jimmy Carter was home. The meeting lasted almost three hours. Carter spoke several times. He blamed himself for the harsh public spotlight focused on the little town and church. He admitted that King was an irrational man. He acknowledged that he had only one vote but that it would be cast voting to rescind the 1965 motion. He would vote to open the church doors to anyone who wanted to enter.

At nearly two o'clock in the afternoon, church clerk Hugh Carter, Jimmy's cousin, a state senator, came to the front steps and read the results of the votes. The congregation had voted 120 to 66 to admit all who wished to attend. It had voted 107 to 84 not to fire Mr. Edwards. It had voted unanimously to create a "watchcare" committee to receive and screen requests for new membership. Plains Baptist, prodded by a waiting public and a new President-elect, had at last opened its doors. Whether King would ever gain membership was still very much in doubt, but services were integrated.

On November 21, King returned and sat in the front row. As the invitation hymn "Jesus Paid It All" was sung, he came forward to apply for membership. He was placed under watchcare. As Jimmy Carter passed him on the way out, King grabbed and kissed the President-elect's hand. He told reporters he would now be a member of the new American Vatican.

He was not to be. The watchcare committee at last recommended, and the congregation concurred, that he be denied membership. He was not a Baptist and he was not a resident of Plains. Just after Carter's inaugural, Pastor Edwards was forced to resign for encouraging integration.

What is so interesting about Plains's public scandal is that a man from such a background, with such roots, a man who still lives and worships there, who still claims it as his home and his church and its

113

people as his family and friends, could be elected President of the United States. More interesting still is the fact that his margin of victory was black. He lost the white vote 51 percent to 47 percent. He won the black vote 87 percent to 13 percent. The black vote was responsible for his victories in Ohio, Pennsylvania, Missouri, Texas, Maryland, Louisiana, and Mississippi. Yet he was from the Deep South, a member of a segregated church in a small south Georgia town.

How did he do it? How did such a man from such a place convince black and liberal white America to vote for him?

Part of the answer is the very fact that Carter is, without any attempt to apologize for the fact, a southerner. He is a southerner who has won the respect and support of his region although differing with some of its basic assumptions. He is able to communicate a kind of warmth that perhaps no other region's liberal can match. He knows blacks and they know him, and they trust him as they cannot trust any northerner, regardless of how liberal that person may be. He is religious in a southern way, and both blacks and white liberals find this attractive.

But thousands of white southerners who claim to be Christians are despised by the very people who voted for Carter. Carter had to prove that while he held all the positive virtues of the southerner, he was not a typical southerner. He had to prove that unlike the other famous, infamous southern headliners of the last quarter century he was neither incendiary nor dumb. He had to prove that despite a slow start and a few atavistic false steps he was at heart no Snopes.

Strom Thurmond, Orval Faubus, George Wallace, Lester Maddox, and a legion of others, despite their individual temperaments, were and are merely rude variations, accidental and minor deviations, on the same old Snopes theme. Ab, Lump, Flem, or Montgomery Ward, they were all, like Strom, Orval, George, or Lester, progenitor and progeny of that same parasitic, pyrotechnic clan from Lower Frenchman's Bend, running amok over decent, civilized folk as they squirmed their way out of primeval kudzic ooze to quasi-respectability in Jefferson. Carter had to prove no kinship with them.

All of this is probably terribly confusing to anyone who has never studied the South and its mythology, particularly the version of it found in the writings of William Faulkner, Dixie's Hesiod. Faulkner considered himself an aristocrat and thus tended to disdain all the poor whites pushing their way up from a bondage as oppressive and unrelieved as that imposed on southern blacks; but even he made a distinction between Bundrens, the noble poor whites, those used and abused by the natural order and the corruptions of petty capitalism, and the abused but also abusing Snopeses, those who took not only from the wealthy Varners and aristocratic Compsons but from the equally needy Bundrens as well.

Faulkner wrote three books about his fictitious
115

but typically southern Snopeses: *The Hamlet, The Town,* and *The Mansion.* The Snopeses were poor white trash—even the name tells us that—who through taking advantage of the weaknesses of wealthier southerners climb up to power over their fellowmen. The most famous of the Snopeses, aside from Ike the Idiot, who loved a cow, were Flem and Mink. Flem, sexually impotent but ruthlessly cunning, tramped in hobnail boots over everyone, including other Snopeses, to win control over the Jefferson bank. He represented to Faulkner the South's new industrial capitalism and the bourgeois class taking power from antebellum planters. Flem was stopped, killed, only by another Snopes, Mink to be precise, whom Flem had let go to prison without extending even a gesture of brotherhood.

Strom, Orval, George, and Lester, all Snopeses, used the convenient fear of race-mixing, a fear now apparently as strong in the North as it was in the South at their rise, to get a leg up in politics, giving little thought to the harvest of the violence they were sowing. Carter, on the other hand, has used racial fear very little in his career, a bit on his way up to governor of Georgia and perhaps just a bit with "ethnic purity" in the primaries; and he used it not at all in the general election. He therefore represents a new phenomenon in American politics, a southern politician who is not a Snopes.

Yet as one reflects on the circumstances of Carter's nomination and then his election to the Presidency, it is clear that his road to victory was paved as much by a quarter century of Strom, Orval,

George, and Lester as by his own considerable talents. That bunch raised such a storm, calling attention to the South's and the nation's racial problems in such abrasive style, that the rest of us were better able to see in Carter a positive solution to the crisis. After Faubus and Maddox it was a relief to find a smart southerner; after Thurmond and Wallace it was a pleasure to find a decent one. After decades of upheaval it was inspiring to find one who offered to help put out the fire the Snopeses had started.

Superficially all the well-known southern politicians, the Snopeses, have the same backgrounds. All but Lester are small-town boys. All but Orval grew up surrounded by Negroes. All but Strom progressed beyond native conservatism to be almost progressive on certain issues. Of the lot, Carter oddly enough has most in common with Wallace, the most racist of them all. They both grew up in fairly comfortable homes, in families that claimed the status of midiminimal village aristocracy, in communities where all of life, except schools and churches, was thoroughly integrated. Why is Wallace a Snopes and Carter a Mallison?

Perhaps it is necessary to look closer at Carter's history. What made him different?

Some say, Carter among them, that it was his mother who set the example of tolerance that he would follow. She is and apparently always was a remarkable woman. To have been racially tolerant in pre-Johnson south Georgia was rare; to have had a Negro visit in your home, to come right in by the front door and sit in the living room and frighten

117

the neighbors by drinking tea, was unheard of. Yet she did such things. Not often perhaps, and not with just any Negro, but with one special young black man who came by to share with her his latest social and academic triumphs in college.

Carter's father did not share such enthusiasms. He is said to have left through the back door as the student knocked at the front. Local blacks knew Earl Carter well enough not to cheer when Joe Louis manhandled Max Schmeling, not until they were out of sight of Earl Carter's house, where they had listened to the fight as Carter's radio beamed it out to them under the trees in the yard. Even the locally based tri-state black Episcopal bishop, the father of that black student of Miss Lillian's, a man Earl Carter respected, one with whom he prayed, played the proper "good nigger" role to satisfy his white friend's very white ego.

To what extent in this ideological struggle between mother and father Miss Lillian guided Jimmy away from paternal and later fraternal racism is something perhaps only a Doris Kearns will ever be able to say for sure; but it is safe to say that Carter's classmates in school, those without such mothers, have shown little inclination toward humanistic enlightenment over the years. Some of his old buddies were off in Americus as late as 1966, when Carter was struggling to be governor, stirring up a race riot that helped elect Lester Maddox. But it is unlikely that even Miss Lillian, a woman radical enough to fear Klan retaliation against her grandchildren, could alone have made Jimmy a liberal on civil rights had he not "gone away to college."

"Going away to college" means for southerners formal schooling or a job away from home that tears them loose from the shelter and safety of local codes. It is a traumatic experience, for it forces them to see life differently. Carter's schooling, first at a regional college, then at Georgia Tech, then at the Naval Academy, demonstrates a decided preference for sciences over liberal arts, the field that usually shakes up southern prejudices the most. At Annapolis there were few blacks. The same was true in the Navy generally. But ten years away from the South, in school, in the Pacific, in New England, had their effect.

The effect was somewhat slow in taking shape. Carter returned to the South in 1953 with the enlightenment that comes with perspective. It took him ten years to build up the wealth and prestige necessary to reveal his broadened vision locally. It took him nearly twenty to arrive at the place where he could do anything statewide. He even "Snopesed" a bit to get where he had to be to do something constructive about racial relations in the South. But he made it at last.

Carter resigned his commission and came home just after his father died in 1953. He took his father's place in the family business and in society and church. His wife bitterly opposed the decision, but in those days before women had rights his word was final.

During the next twenty years, as Carter rebuilt

the family fortune, trained his brother Billy to run it, and turned his attention to ever higher office, he kept his racial attitudes pretty much to himself. He did vote to keep his church's doors open to blacks. He weathered a minor boycott by the "good old boys" by refusing to join a newly organized chapter of the White Citizens Council. South Georgia was in flames, and he said little either way as he ran for office.

After a heated race against corruption in government, Carter entered the Georgia senate in 1963. There he worked hard but cautiously. Only once, when he helped block state aid to a segregated white academy in his home county, did he make any significant racial stand. He worked on economic improvements that would help Negroes as well as whites, but he said little that would associate him with racism or liberalism.

In 1966 he ran for governor. He never led the pack. Cartoons in the Atlanta *Constitution* showed him in a crowded field of followers, tumbling along behind Lester Maddox and Bo Callaway. He talked mostly of fiscal integrity and honesty in government. He refused to bait blacks, but he did not call for greater civil rights. Lester Maddox, winning with a racist campaign, did not tempt him. Carter, running behind but close enough to have hope, might have pictured himself the George Wallace of Georgia, but he did not. He lost.

As soon as the 1966 race was over, he began planning for 1970. He campaigned for four years. He won. He won partly because he had decided at the first of the year to run as a redneck, the South's code word for racist.

In his autobiography Carter blames his image in the race of 1970 on the Atlanta *Constitution*. "The editor early in the campaign began to characterize me as an ignorant and bigoted redneck peanut farmer," he wrote. "Editorial cartoons showed me standing in the muck of racism while all the other candidates disappeared into the sunrise of enlightenment." But from all other indications, the blame or credit for this image, a winning one in Georgia in 1970, was as much Carter's as the media's. He told a reporter at the beginning of the year that he would purposely run as a "local Georgia conservative Democrat. . . . I'm basically a redneck." He later explained that this simply meant he would speak for those who had no support from special interests; it had no racial connotation. But Carter was aware of what he said. He knew what he was doing. While he never spoke disparagingly of blacks, he let racist Georgians know he was the alternative to "liberal" former governor Carl Sanders.

Steven Brill in his *Harper's* article recounts the "sins" of Carter's 1970 campaign. It is hard to tell how accurately the media covered Carter, since as one special interest they were supporting Sanders, but enough can be traced to Carter to see that his enlightened record is not pure. He tried to identify Sanders with ultraliberals such as Hubert Humphrey. He defended the state's right-to-work law, which he said the liberal Sanders, big labor's friend, wanted to repeal. He denied having said the Supreme Court's desegregation order was morally and legally right. He promised if elected to invite George Wallace of Alabama to speak to the Georgia legislature. He permitted his organization to distribute a picture of Sanders celebrating a basketball victory with two black Atlanta Hawks and a bottle of champagne, a fairly typical Dixie dirty trick of the day.

He helped finance the campaign of a black running for governor, hoping he might siphon off some of Sanders' black votes. Just before the primary in September, he visited an all-white private high school academy and assured whites that as governor he would always approve of private education. (He would later say he saw them merely as safety valves against a racial explosion in a period of transition.) He won only 7 percent of the black vote, but he did win the poor-white vote, and he won the nomination. He went on to be elected governor in November.

During the general election, he embraced Lester Maddox, who as retiring governor had been nominated lieutenant governor on the Democratic ticket. He said he was proud to run on the same slate with a man who so well represented the essence of Democratic philosophy. Such sentiment (Carter later said he only meant Lester was so much better than the Republican opposition) contradicted that of Atlanta's former progressive mayor Ivan Allen and Charles Weltner, a U. S. Representative from Atlanta who gave up his seat in 1966 rather than run on a ticket headed by Maddox. It also contradicted Carter's own statements about Maddox after the election and especially during the 1976 election when, after Lester had called him a liar, he said: "Being called a liar by Lester Maddox is like being called ugly by a frog."

His redneck campaign got him elected. The "racist" peanut farmer from Plains was governor. Why did he run such a campaign? Some say he simply did what he had to do to be elected. He had lost to racists in 1966. He would not do so again. If he had to run as a redneck, if as Wallace said in 1959 he had to "out-niggah" them, so be it. Perhaps.

Others say he played a part, pretended to be what he was not, used dirty tricks, lowered himself, in order to be elected so he could then do something to help the very people he lost in the primary. The needs of blacks and poor whites in Georgia are quite similar. They are both at odds with the wealthy, whom Carter believed Sanders really favored. He could not come out for the blacks because they were not enough to win and because coming out for them would alienate the very poor whites who were enough to win. This was one of the ambiguities politicians constantly face. He had to do wrong, to pretend a racism he never felt, to do right.

Once safely elected, with only the Presidency above him in ambition, he could at last say the things he had felt all along. Not a few conservatives and liberals, both of whom expected him to be racist, were caught short when they heard his inaugural address on the occasion of being sworn in as governor:

> At the end of a long campaign, I believe I know the people of this state as well as anyone. Based on this knowledge of Georgians north and south, rural and urban, liberal and conservative, I say to you quite frankly that the time for racial discrimination is over. Our people have already made this major and difficult decision, but we cannot underestimate the challenge of hundreds of minor decisions yet to be made. Our inherent human charity and our religious beliefs will be taxed to the limit. No poor, rural, weak, or black person should ever have to bear the additional burden of being deprived of the opportunity of an education, a job, or simple justice.

Then he decided to hang pictures of distinguished black Georgians next to those of distinguished white Georgians in the state capitol building. One of the honored was Nobel Laureate Dr. Martin Luther King, Jr. This caused a great outcry of protest, led by Lester Maddox, who swore when he was governor again he would take it down. But Carter, the stubborn "south Georgia mud turtle," went right ahead with his plan. He was then hailed in the national press as a true representative of the new South.

It is of course just possible that he was playing a part both times, the redneck to get elected governor of Georgia, the enlightened progressive because he had higher goals in mind. No one doubts his ambition—or his skills as an actor. While orchestrating the anti-McGovern movement at the 1972 Democratic National Convention, he worked behind the scenes to be chosen McGovern's vice-presidential choice. United States Congressman Andrew Young reported on NBC's *Meet the Press* on July 18, 1976, that while Governor Carter pretended sympathy for segregationists, he worked secretly with black leaders in the state to bring Georgia "out of the Dark Ages." Who then is Jimmy Carter? Is he or is he not a Snopes? In the South, where he learned to give complicated answers to all questions, where he learned the art of fuzzing, a leader's merit must be judged by acts and not words. By this standard Carter is no Snopes.

In 1976 the Jimmy Carter that Americans decided to elect their President appeared. He was many things. Though a former governor, he was an outsider, a nonpolitician, one of us. He was honest ("I'll never lie to you") and compassionate. He had a big smile. He was born again. He was no Snopes. He made a big issue of separating himself politically from George Wallace. He said over and over that the Supreme Court decision of 1954 was the best thing to happen to his part of the country in a generation.

Some observers, knowing a bit about Carter's history, were skeptical. Some found reason for skepticism in his campaign itself. David Broder wrote in *The Washington Post* on March 31 that Carter was either "the most promising political figure of the 70's" or "the most skillful demagogue." He had followed Carter around from speech to speech, from a rally with blacks to one with whites. Carter had won over both groups. His speech was basically the same both places, except that he changed critical words and omitted critical sentences, creating a different tone each place, so that both groups thought he was on their side. Carter was trying to stand tall on both sides of the fence. Something was wrong somewhere. Broder failed to see that as President, Carter would have to do just that.

Ken Bode, writing for *New Republic* a week later, puzzled over Carter's black support. Surely blacks must know he is against busing. They must see that he speaks to no specifically black issues. All he has is a smile and a shoeshine and a patriotic sermon. What Bode failed to consider is that black Americans respond to smiles and shoeshines and patriotic sermons the same way whites do, perhaps more so, given their ministerial tradition. They simply trusted Carter. But Bode concluded that Carter's black support was simply anti-Wallace support, that blacks would leave Carter after he finished Wallace off in Dixie. Bode was wrong.

The one thing that pundits could neither understand nor explain was the continuing support of black Congressman Andrew Young. He was the key to Carter's black support. He was unshakable in his resolve. Why? Was he, an ordained minister, fooled by Carter's religious pose? Did he want a cabinet job that badly? Young attempted to explain his position in an article for *The Nation.* He said that blacks have always recognized as their best allies those southern whites who stay at home and run the risk of persecution by working for racial and economic justice. Carter had grown up in a town where blacks outnumbered whites four hundred to three hundred and had not "Snopesed" in office. Ignoring the 1970 primary, Young pointed to Carter's positive racial record as governor, especially his decision to make every high school principal in the state a voting registrar to assure that more citizens, black and white, get registered to vote. Carter was his man. Young brought with him Atlanta's black establishment, the nation's most visible and respected, and they in turn brought black America.

Then came April, the press conference in Indianapolis, and the ethnic purity statement. Carter told newsmen that while he supported open-housing laws, he opposed the government's injecting blacks into white neighborhoods just to integrate them. He certainly did not oppose any neighborhood's decision to keep itself ethnically pure.

The statement caused an uproar among blacks and panic in the Carter camp. Outsiders said that at last he had shown his real redneck colors. Carter at first refused to retreat. The liberal candidates had said the same thing. Why weren't they being scored for it? After a week, seeing his precious black support sliding, he gave in. He apologized. Daddy King forgave him. Blacks voted for him 87 percent to 13 percent in November.

Carter owes his election to black America. They should be favored in his administration. Andrew Young is the first black to be U.S. Ambassador to the United Nations. Other blacks will hold key positions. Carter will appoint a black, perhaps a black woman, to the Supreme Court. Like Lyndon Johnson before him, he may well be remembered most for what he did for minority America. Perhaps Young will be proven right. Perhaps an enlightened southerner *is* the black man's best bet.

While much was made of Carter's religious faith during the primaries, no one seemed to connect it with Carter's enlightenment on racial matters. Southern religion has been so defamed by politicians pretending piosity that hardly anyone recognized its civilizing effect on someone who really took it seriously.

Carter has never said that his faith made him a racial liberal. He has said it makes him care for people, all people. It is not unlikely that the ethics he learned in church, the faith that condemns division and hatred whether it be in first-century Palestine or the twentieth-century South, helped him see the dangers of racism.

We must of course be careful not to suggest that everyone who claims Christian convictions and attends church is automatically enlightened. Not everyone who sits through Baptist sermons learns about love. All four of the Snopeses mentioned earlier are "virtuous" by their own lights. Strom Thurmond is one of the most "religious" politicians in America. He reads his Bible nightly. Hardly a Sunday passes that he does not preach in some right-wing Protestant church against the evils of godless communism. A devout "Christian" and a committed racist, he sees no conflict of interest.

Orval Faubus, according to Robert Sherrill in *Gothic Politics in the Deep South*, considered a ministerial career before settling on politics. He once demonstrated his religious convictions by sheltering a Holiness family in the Arkansas governor's mansion when they risked arrest by refusing to comply with a state law requiring schoolchildren to be vaccinated against smallpox. He claimed to consult God personally about every decision he made as governor, and he said the decision to call out the National Guard to enforce segregation at Little Rock Central in 1957 came after much prayer. Perhaps the truest Snopes of them all, Orval was no racist in his early career. Raised in the Ozarks, where he seldom even saw a black person, he turned racist only when he needed a hot issue to win a third term. His faith held up no warning hand.

Lester Maddox also considered the ministry. He still preaches in as many as three churches on a given Sunday. He found support in Holy Writ for his segregationist policies while governor of Georgia. The ax handles with which he kept blacks out of his Pickrick Restaurant in Atlanta could just as well have been crude wooden crosses.

Among the Snopeses, only Wallace exhibits little religious fervor. Wallace's grandfather, a rural doctor, did try to make a preacher of his bright little grandson, but according to Marshall Frady in *Wallace* the scheme failed, fortunately perhaps for all concerned, especially the church. Religion has little effect on Wallace. To his credit he uses it little.

Carter is different. He is not above letting his constituents know about it. He perhaps uses it a bit too much. But it seems to be genuine. It has helped elevate his mind. It has taught him to love everyone. It has kept him from being a Snopes—most of the time.

Chapter VII

Millennium:
The Carter "Reign"

JIMMY CARTER'S MOTHER, Miss Lillian, recently referred in an interview with *Ms.* magazine to certain of her expectations during "Jimmy's reign." Considering the "royalist" tendencies of the last few American Presidents, perhaps the term, though a slip, was not so misplaced; but it does seem a bit out of keeping for the administration of a candidate pledged to the abolition of the "imperial" Presidency. Carter tried to reverse the Nixon imagery, tried to restore perhaps a Jacksonian style by walking part of the way to the White House after the inaugural. He wore a sweater for his first televised fireside chat. He has cut back on the number of big black limousines available for government employees. He stayed in a private home on one trip to Massachusetts and made his own bed. But then Miss Lillian just might know something we will know only with time.

What sort of Presidency can we expect from the peanut farmer and Southern Baptist Sunday school teacher from south Georgia? If Carter is reelected in 1980, if he confounds at long last the curse of

Tecumseh which has taken the life in office of every President elected in a zero year since William Henry Harrison, Carter will "reign" until 1984. What kind of America will this most overtly Christian of Presidents leave behind after an eight-year tenure ending on George Orwell's predicted date for total governmental mind control? Will 1984 be doomsday or the opening days of the millennium? Or will it simply be the end of another average President's term, with a weary Carter, elder statesman, playing Ike to his loyal Mondale? Will things be better or worse in the land of the free and the home of the brave? How much better, or how much worse?

No one knows. But one thing we can predict with certainty is that Carter, like each of our other recent Presidents, will leave a lasting and distinctive mark on the office. After Roosevelt, a President could hardly fail to respond vigorously to national crises. After Truman, a President could hardly fail— though some tried—to share with the people his major plans for national and international strategy. After Eisenhower, a President could not fail to fly off occasionally for summit conferences. After Kennedy, a President could not fail to use the mass media to marshal public support for his political programs. After Johnson, a President could not neglect, except benignly, the needs of minorities. Nixon and Ford have been gone too short a time for us to judge accurately their effects on the office, but we may be sure they will be lasting. The same will be true of Carter.

Each President has worked through an image.

132

Roosevelt was the country squire, the patrician, the man whose *noblesse oblige* ordered him back into public life after paralysis, who served his country from a wheelchair when life as a retiring gentleman would have been easier. Truman was the poor but honest small-town clerk, the pillar of society, capable of lofty ideas and great deeds yet still favorably disposed to street-corner humor and fits of fatherly temper when someone insulted his little girl's operatic pretensions. Eisenhower was the general, spit and polish with a heart of gold, a grandfather right out of a Shirley Temple movie, perfectly cast for the silent but disturbed '50s. Kennedy was youth and clear-eyed idealism. Johnson was patriotic prairie populism. Nixon was tormented, amoral competence. Ford was a good old boy. Such stereotypes are, of course, sometimes unfair, sometimes cruel, often inaccurate; but to a great extent they are the creations of the men who bore them, and they endure. Jimmy Carter, whether we are comfortable with the image or not, is the preacher. He devised the image, it stuck, and now we must all live with it.

It is by this image that he will conduct his Presidential business. It will be the standard by which we as historians and citizens will judge him.

In his acceptance speech in July 1976 he was the Baptist evangelist. In his inaugural address in January 1977 he was the Baptist pastor.

After an invocation and "religious" preliminaries, after the "laying on of hands" by the chief justice, "Reverend" Carter, the new minister, turned to his congregation, his new charge of 212,000,000,

133

and read his text. It was taken from the Old Testament—from Micah 6:8: "And what doth the Lord require of thee, but to do justly, and to love mercy, and to walk humbly with thy God?"

He said this was his first duty as pastor. He said it was the duty of every citizen-member. This day, this inaugural, marked a new beginning, a new birth, a rebirth, a rededication to an old dream, the birth of a new spirit to help carry it out. That dream, first conceived by the nation's founders, was one of Biblical justice and mercy, those things that God requires of his people. The dream is being reborn today. To accomplish it, we must walk humbly with God, as the Founding Fathers did.

For Jimmy Carter, great-grandson of Puritans, America was born on the *Mayflower*. It would be reborn when the *Mayflower* ideals of justice and mercy within a community under God were revived. This could be the moment.

The first sermon was appropriately short. It simply listed the goals of the new administration. Barriers separating men one from another must go down. Productive work must be provided for everyone capable of work. There must be stronger family ties, better laws, and governmental competence that will make people proud of their system. With the help of God, amen.

Again, as in Madison Square Garden, as in whistle-stops all over the country, the style and vocabulary were ministerial. Carter as President will be the preacher, perhaps pastor now more than evangelist, but still preacher. His image will reflect upon the church and faith he represents.

Back in the spring of 1976, during the days just preceding the Pennsylvania primary, Carter granted an interview to *World Mission Journal*. It is perhaps the clearest, most concise statement of his goals as a pastoral President: "I would try to exemplify in every moment of my life those attitudes and actions of Christianity that I believe in. I would ask God for guidance on decisions affecting our country and make those decisions after evaluating the alternatives as best I could. I would recognize that my influence on others would be magnified a hundred times over as President." He would pray, he would use his God-given reason, he would be careful to use his influence wisely. Very ministerial.

There is of course an element of the ministerial image in every President. Perhaps it is simply a part of the civilized, Christianized American male's psyche. Perhaps what we call "ministerial" is just the Western male's culturally conditioned fatherly, husbandly, brotherly personality. Roosevelt had it. So did Truman and Eisenhower, Kennedy and Johnson, even Nixon and Ford. To exhort, to chasten, to comfort, to inspire, all these are both ministerial and Presidential. But Jimmy Carter's ministerialism is thicker, deeper, creamier than any we have known. He will truly be pastor of the American church.

He will, as he promised over and over in the campaign, act as a Christian President. Translated, this means he will always try to do what he considers the Christian thing. His religious principles are not as

135

vague as those of most Presidents. He is a specific kind of religious person, a specific kind of Christian, a specific kind of Baptist. He will be those things, he will reflect their training, he will in turn reflect upon them. What he does as President, fair or not, will show us what Baptists in particular have done to train potential leaders to conduct political business in a fashion befitting a disciple of Christ. Jimmy Carter, believing as he does that politics is ministry, agreeing with Teddy Roosevelt that the Presidency is a bully pulpit, stubborn as the proverbial Georgia mud turtle about following his principles, may well tell us more than we have ever known about Southern Baptist religious education.

To study Carter closely is to see at least four distinctive characteristics typical of contemporary Southern Baptist leadership. He is what we are. He is what we have produced in a President.

One, to our credit, Carter promises to be a compassionate leader. He has been influenced by the liberal movements in recent political and religious life more than most Christians, certainly more than most Southern Baptists, but he thinks very much like the more sensitive and enlightened members of our denomination. He will therefore propose legislation aimed at helping the disenfranchised and downtrodden. He will push programs to rescue and rehabilitate groups lost in the great American press for economic progress. He will both preach and practice the social gospel. This will be true on the international as well as the domestic scene, as his threat to cut aid to nations abusing human rights,

Russia as well as Uganda, indicates. This emphasis on human rights, already emerging, could be his most important single crusade.

Two, he will effectively dramatize his programs. Like all southern leaders, political and religious, Baptists in particular, he will be a good actor. The ancient Greeks called their actors "hypocrites," and many Americans, influenced by the modern connotation of that word, consider political acting hypocrisy. We like acting on the stage and screen but not on the stump and certainly not in the White House. But it is very important that a President be a good actor. He should not of course be a hypocrite in the modern sense of the word. He should not mask his true feelings or dealings with a good false act. He should, however, use his considerable talents to convince the public that his programs are right. He should, like a good pastor, dramatize through words and deeds his important messages. Carter, who so effectively personified and dramatized honesty and integrity as a candidate, should as President use the grease paint to good purpose.

Three, he will try to administer an "open" Presidency. He has promised to do so. He takes great pride in the new "sunshine" laws of his governorship. He has promised to keep the American public informed of his thinking and decisions on important domestic and foreign matters—even to the point of opening heretofore closed cabinet meetings to the press.

This would of course be true to his Baptist heritage. Among Baptists, the pastor, the deacons, the

137

trustees, even Sunday school teachers are responsible to the congregation. They must look to the people for power, and these leaders must therefore keep the people informed and answer their questions. This is the essence of democracy, political or religious, and it is the ideal toward which Carter should drive. We can only hope that he is not sidetracked by the hard reality of power politics, as many Baptist pastors have been.

Fourth, and perhaps most significantly, he will be pragmatic. As the one distinctively American philosophy, pragmatism—practicality, to do the possible, to make things work—has influenced politics and religion as much as it has influenced business and industry. First articulated by William James and Charles Sanders Peirce, it has been filtered through the minds of such diverse men as John Dewey, Booker T. Washington, and Harry Truman. It may at times have drained away some of our idealism, but it has also warned us away from disastrous ideological pitfalls. It may well have helped us to reach goals without fully realizing what we have done. Deceptive but most effective, pragmatism is a useful tool for the compassionate actor at the head of state.

Carter, pragmatic enough to get himself elected governor of Georgia and President of the United States, might well remind us of a modern minister as he looks for ways to make his compassionate goals workable. Like the Texas Baptists who recently hired a Dallas Jewish agency to make their television commercials for Christ, like the theologian who let an atheist doctor with a good record remove his tumor but who did his own praying, Carter will do "the Christian thing" in a very practical manner.

For this reason, his greatest accomplishments, whatever they may be, might not be recognized until he has long since departed the scene. The pragmatic actor could just slip things by us. He seems to have chosen a rather undistinguished cabinet, more "mules" than "thoroughbreds," no Kissingers or Moynihans, no great innovators, just efficient mechanics to make Carter's plans work. We may for a time think things are dull—until we see what the preacher has done.

Carter will need all his Baptist ministerial skills in the days ahead. A number of pressing issues will doubtless tax his compassion, his dramatic ingenuity, and his practical sense. One of these, the one he seems to have made his first and central goal, the one that demonstrates his primal passion for pastoral efficiency, is the reorganization of the federal government.

No one disagrees with Carter that the federal bureaucracy is clumsy and wasteful. Such a reorganization was in fact the major goal of the second Nixon Administration before Watergate opened up and swept everything away in its flood. The myriad departments and agencies with all their duties make the average American want to throw up his hands in despair. Carter, like a new pastor, wants to prune and consolidate this hydra, to make it work better, to make it less oppressive if not less costly.

He says he can trim federal agencies from nineteen hundred to two hundred. He says he trimmed agencies in Georgia from three hundred to twenty-two. Critics point out, however, that at the end of his four years as governor Georgia had 30 percent more state employees operating under a 50 percent higher budget. Carter counters that he had promised only a more efficient government, not one less expensive or smaller. Those who work for the government, those benefiting from government programs, those who believe government's chief role is to be the protection of the unfortunate, need not fear a Carter Presidency nearly so much as those who detest paying taxes. Carter is a liberal Democrat, different from many others only in his love of efficiency. As long as government is doing its job well, he will not worry about its size or cost.

He will then be judged by his own standards. He himself has made the reorganization an issue, perhaps the most important issue of his first administration. He intends to rework, for the sake of the people, an institution originally designed to help the people but now grown fat and lazy with age and indulgence. History will decide how well he did with it.

To succeed he will have to work well with Congress. Can he do this? He did not, all who watched agreed, work well with the Georgia legislature. He came to office with certain goals, the legislature usually balked, and he refused to compromise. While there is no shame in failing to see eye to eye with a body that once refused to seat Julian Bond because he disagreed with American policy in Vietnam, it could be a signal that Carter will have trouble working with any Congress that refuses to grant him all the powers he needs to reorganize and carry out programs he wants.

At the moment, he is lucky to have a Democratic Congress anxious after eight years of Republican vetoes to work with a President of their own party. He will have to take advantage of this initial goodwill because history says it will not long endure. He will also have to learn to compromise. Otherwise we could have a political church divided—like Baptists —by a fuss between pastor and deacons.

Carter will also need all his Baptist pastoral skills in dealing with another pressing issue, one that he agreed during the campaign was urgent, one he promised to solve, a declining economy.

By "getting America moving again" he does not mean, as Presidents before him have meant, increasing useless production. Still deeply influenced by what he considers the rich natural texture of a poor boy's childhood, he seems not to mourn the passing of America's recent age of conspicuous consumption. He speaks almost with anticipation of a time when Americans will once again live simple lives, uncluttered by too many things, more peaceful after years of frantic pursuit of gilded pleasures. He is, in a word, old-fashioned.

When he speaks of economic recovery, he means jobs. He is pledged, and he apparently intends to

141

keep his pledge, to put Americans back to work. He prefers that they work for private industry, but if he has to make work for them, he will. As a member of a church noted for keeping its members constantly busy, as a personal friend and softball team mate of Ralph Nader, he seems to feel that a high standard of wasteful living is far less important than constructive labor.

He has said, "I believe in the work ethic." He has expanded on this by saying, "I believe that anyone who is able to work ought to work—and have a chance to work." Notice the word "believe." It is a matter of faith. The chance to work should be guaranteed by a compassionate government, one that sees it must train workers to be self-sufficient rather than be eternally dependent on it. Carter is a particular kind of liberal. He believes the government should intervene in society to help people, especially to help them find useful employment, but that the help should be designed to make them independent. He is fond of quoting the Chinese philosopher Kuan Tzu: "If you give a man a fish, he has one meal. If you teach him how to fish, he can feed himself for life." A compassionate government will educate workers for life.

The work ethic that Carter so proudly espouses was once called the Protestant ethic after Max Weber's thesis that exploitative capitalism grew out of bourgeois Protestant morality which extolled work as holy worship. Weber of course conveniently overlooked the fact that capitalism was born in Catholic Renaissance Italy, but certain facts did

142

tend to substantiate his thesis that the work ethic came to fullest maturity in Protestant theology. Capitalism and its work ethic, its contention that God favors and rewards those who work hard and save their money, was stronger in northern (Protestant) Europe than in the south, and stronger in Protestant-Puritan America than anywhere in Europe. There was even some evidence that certain early Protestant leaders, John Calvin among them, had taught that God's chosen people were those who worked hard and saved their capital for future investment.

Carter, a Baptist-Puritan, believes that work is good for people. He intends to reverse the Rooseveltian trend, which has put so many needy people on public welfare roles, by making it possible for them to work. This will be their salvation. It is the pastor's job to make salvation available.

Hard work has certainly paid off for Carter. His life reads like a Southern Baptist sermon illustration. His "Gospel of Peanuts" tells of a barefoot boy from south Georgia who through hard work earned high marks in the Naval Academy and the rank of lieutenant in the active Navy. This boy, disturbed by the death of a father who had worked hard and earned the respect of his town, suddenly gave up his commission to return home and raise peanuts. Again hard work paid off. He made money. He became a leading citizen of his town. He earned a place of leadership. He was elected state senator, then governor, then President of the United States.

It took Spartan (Puritan, Baptist) discipline. Next

to his father, Carter says he most admires Admiral Rickover, his superior in the Navy. The "impersonal demands of a perfectionist" have stayed with him through the years. One interview with this disciplined sage gave the title to Carter's book *Why Not the Best?* when Rickover showed obvious disappointment that Carter had not always done his best, had not always worked as hard as possible, had not always reached his potential. Carter says the only personality trait he carried with him from the Navy was self-discipline. It has obviously paid off. He believes it pays off for everyone. He believes that Americans have been disciplined by Vietnam and Watergate and the failure of the current welfare system. He wants to put America back to work. He will use liberal techniques to accomplish conservative goals. He will be, as Franklin Roosevelt once said of himself, a liberal because he is at heart a conservative.

Carter will also have to deal, at home and abroad, with the problems of minorities and oppressed majorities. He has made it clear that like a good Baptist pastor he will do so.

Just after his nomination in July, he was invited to a California party given by movie and television stars to show their support. He was friendly to them, but he shocked them by making it plain that they were not the kind of people he wanted to be President to help. He would take their campaign money and thank them for their help, but as President he would try to help those who really needed him. He was running in the only race where all the people make the big decision. If elected, he would defend the have-nots.

Noble words, but what do they mean? We must assume that among those he expected to help most are black and brown minorities. They assured his victory. They have the right to demand a return. He seems ready to give it. Just what he will give is not clear. Naming Griffin Bell to the Department of Justice was a real jolt for many blacks, especially for northern blacks who saw him simply as a redneck judge who had stayed popular in the South through the '60s. But southern blacks, who supported Carter long before the alternative to Gerald Ford turned northern blacks into believers, came to Bell's defense. He had to be judged, as did Carter, in the light of the obstacles he faced in the racist South. He had done more, given his circumstances, than most northern liberals. He would, given the freedom of Washington, do much more. The nomination was apparently not the disaster it was first thought to be.

Griffin Bell's nomination was, however, unexpected; and it caused quite a stir in black communities. So too, for the opposite reason, did the nomination of Andrew Young as ambassador to the United Nations. Congressman Young, black and winning, committed to fundamental changes in American policy toward underdeveloped nations, promised to be a powerful and at times discomfiting force in the Carter cabinet. He has kept his word.

Young has been especially well received by the second group having the right to expect Carter's help, the emerging black nations of Africa. Believing as he does that "racism is a greater threat to world peace than communism," Young will doubtless take a strong stand for majority rule around the globe and for peaceful and just revolution. Black African diplomats have made it clear that they regard him as an American first and a black man second, but they are pleased by his nomination. White Africans feel quite differently. Should he be able to withstand the criticism and abuse he will receive as the most individualistic of the Administration team, he might last long enough to be the thoroughbred among the Carter mules.

But perhaps the most important group that will come to Carter for the help he promised them will be that great American oppressed minority, the women of the country. Carter says he will respond. He says he wants to be to women what Lyndon Johnson was to blacks. He has appointed two women to his cabinet and has pledged to name many others to positions where they can be trained for higher places in the future. He has begun a quiet drive to put Presidential pressure on several states where a vote on the Equal Rights Amendment to the Constitution is soon to rise.

It is hard to say just what Carter, deep inside, thinks of women. He admits he finds them physically attractive. He tends to show them southern gentlemanly deference and indulgent tolerance. He seems to associate them with compassion and softness, while associating men with discipline and toughness. This is of course his heritage, as it is that

146

of most middle-aged American men. But intellectually he knows better. He has referred many times, once in his inaugural address, to the educational leadership and inspiration of his teacher Miss Julia Coleman. He was deeply impressed by his mother's two-year service in the Peace Corps in India. His wife, Rosalynn, as tough as they come, has shown him the metallic side of the female personality. A journalistic lip-reader at the Democratic National Convention and an open microphone at the inauguration amply demonstrated the way she directs her family, including the President, to proper forms of social intercourse.

Carter is a man who has had to overcome some deeply embedded racial and national and sexual prejudices. He has come a long way, farther than most, and he has a long way to go. He was once a southern white man. Now he is President. As pastor of all the people, he will be judged by the distance he travels in his four or eight years. Some will condemn him for not going far enough, some for going too far. Once again it will be the old pastoral dilemma.

He will also be judged by his commitment to and his success in the protection of the environment. The revolting college students of the late '60s, before they were returned to normalcy by gunfire at Kent State, left behind in their rubble the issue of man's treatment of nature. It may have been worth all the trouble.

Carter has promised to protect living things.

More than a few people voted for him because his environmental proposals were superior to the laissez-faire program of Gerald Ford. Carter will have to come through with new laws and strict enforcement of existing laws to keep their faith and support.

In his autobiography he spends a good deal of time describing the delights of rural beauty as he knew it in childhood. He claims environmental protection, reversal of ecological disaster, as one of his greatest achievements as governor of Georgia. He opposes the use of dangerous pesticides. He is particularly cautious about the use of nuclear fuels. There is—as one would expect from a pastor—a theological tone to his statements. This is God's world. It is here to be used but not used up. It is only a small step from believing in the resurrection to believing in the greening of America.

To accomplish all his goals, to be judged a great President, Carter will need more than one four-year term. To win a second term, he will need to strengthen his party. He won by a rather narrow margin in 1976. Six months later it was difficult to find a voter who was not for him. Three years hence it may be difficult to find one who is. Presidential popularity sweeps wildly up and down, and given just a bit of bad luck here and there, Carter could well be on his way down in 1980. It is therefore necessary for him to expand his support, and to do that he will have to patch up a party of contradictions which is at present ready to rip apart at the seams.

The Democrats are in decline today. Seldom if ever can they claim the support of more than 40 percent of the people polled on the street, a far more accurate place to poll them than in a booth on election day when they are forced to choose between two names. They are the majority party. They have all the various "outs" of American society. Democrats are industrial labor, southern blacks and whites, militants of all kinds, the down-and-outs of every color and region. They seldom get the benefit in Congress of being the loyal opposition, of sweeping out an unresponsive old-guard leadership, of having time to catch their breath and think of the future.

Yet they grow smaller, and the fissures that began to show as early as 1948 and continued to expand in 1968 and 1972 grow more pronounced. Carter, who almost put things back together in 1976, must work very hard to restore his party to harmony and true majority. Should he be as little interested in party machinery as most sitting Presidents have been, he might be in for a rude awakening in 1980.

All that keeps the Democrats in power is the perpetual invalidity of its opposition, the Republicans. Since the Depression of the 1930's, this once-majority party has been in rapid decline. There is an occasional scenario for revival, brave talk of a vigorous new Republican leader who will clearly and attractively articulate the "people's philosophy" and

149

restore its credibility. But there will never be a Grand New Party. Its owners want majorities only on election days, not afterward when it's time to cut the pie. They enjoy too much being a rich man's club. They enjoy sitting before their hearty fires drinking toasts to yesterday.

The party system is sick. Carter could be just the prescription it needs. He will need to be bold enough to create strong political support and strong opposition. He promises to be that bold.

He certainly wants to be a strong President. He wants to change things for the good of all the people. He once said: "I think the President ought to be—I think the nation is best served by a President who is strong and aggressive and innovative and sensitive. Working with the Congress. Is strong, independent, in harmony for a change, with mutual respect for a change. In the open, and with a minimum of secrecy for a change. I don't think the Congress is capable of leadership. That's no reflection on the Congress, but you can't have 535 people leading the nation. I don't think the Founding Fathers ever thought that Congress would lead this country. There's only one person in this nation that can speak with a clear voice to the American people. There's only one person that can set a standard of ethics and morality and excellence and greatness or call on the American people to make a sacrifice and explain the purpose of the sacrifice, or answer difficult questions or propose and carry out bold programs, or to provide for defense posture that would make us feel secure, a foreign policy that would make us proud once again, and that's the President." And that's the kind of President he wants to be.

He might be. He will certainly be competent. He will try to move the country the way he thinks it should go. He will do "the Christian thing" with great skill and a dash of the dramatic. He will make things happen.

He will rise or fall by his vision of what America should be. If his vision is strong and good and accurate enough, he will make a great President. If not, he might very well be relegated to a dusty drawer of history. As a national pastor, he naturally sees America in theological colors. We are a sinful people being reborn, being given a second chance. We can, if we try hard enough, create a true righteous community.

Peter Steinfels of *Commonweal* has compared Carter's references to a community inspired by belief in a transcendent reality standing over and behind it to the language used by John Winthrop on the *Mayflower* as the Pilgrims drew up plans for the new Plymouth Colony. "It is a language which has been submerged, at least since Wilson, in the Main Street 'normalcy' of the inter-war Republicans, of Eisenhower and of Ford; in the secular progressivism of the New Deal; in the upwardly mobile urban ethos of the Kennedys; and in the Willy Lomanism of Nixon." With Carter it has been and is being revived. Can he sell it to the American people? Can it mean what it once did? All that can be said is that it is certainly worth a try.

As for Carter himself, he says, "I see an America on the move again, united, a diverse and vital and tolerant nation, entering our third century with pride and confidence—an America that lives up to the majesty of our Constitution and the simple decency of our people." It will not be a homogeneous society in which the rewards of labor are taken from the motivated and given to the poor; but it will be a nation in which the strong brother helps lift up to useful labor his less fortunate brother. The government, led by a strong President somewhat akin to the stern but gentle father of a family, will see to it.

Jimmy Carter's Presidency is still on the loom. It is still to be made. What it proves to be will depend upon Carter himself, upon circumstances beyond his control, and upon God. It will also depend upon the strength and validity of his Baptist heritage. Southern Baptists have now given us a President. True to his tradition, he is a Puritan, a missionary, a democrat. Despite the ambitions of his proud mother, he has promised an end to the imperial Presidency of the past quarter century. In his jeans and sweater, he would seem the long-awaited antidote to the recent trend toward kingship. As a good Baptist pastor, will he be simply the ordained leader of a true congregation? Can the modern Puritan with his democratic ideals and missionary zeal lead the free world into positive and effective programs for future progress? We shall soon see.

Bill Moyers, the thin, bespectacled young Southern Baptist minister who became President Lyndon Johnson's right-hand man in the White House, said in an interview in 1965 that he was not worried about compromising his Christian commitment and testimony by political service. When the federal government is doing the work of the Kingdom of God, he said in effect, there is no reason to stand outside and criticize. He was referring to Johnson's Great Society legislation to help the poor and oppressed. He was not, we may assume, speaking of the policy in Southeast Asia.

Two years later Moyers was desperately struggling to free himself from Johnson and his unpopular government. The Kingdom had fallen. An older, wiser, sadder Moyers still asks liberal politicians how they can be so sure they are doing holy work.

This, in the light of Jimmy Carter's "ministerial" Presidency, makes the thoughtful Christian ask just how supportive of a politician, even one who promises always to do "the Christian thing," he or she should be. Should Christians pray for Carter's success in keeping the peace and avoiding domestic disaster? Of course. Should we refrain from criticizing his mistakes in the hope that his and our Christian image is not tarnished? Of course not. Should we openly support him? Perhaps, but not because he claims to be a Christian, not without moral reservations, and not necessarily as political insiders.

The term "Christian citizen" has always been somewhat self-contradictory. It has caused many people quite a lot of anguish. Since Christ founded his church as a forerunning testimony to the coming Kingdom, as a movement designed essentially to announce the rapid demise of the world order,

73

Christians have from earliest times found it hard to be good citizens. They have respected "the powers that be" as powers ordained of God. They have rendered to Caesar the things that are Caesar's. But they have at best kept their distance. They have wanted as little as possible to do with a society whose days are numbered.

Now, two thousand years since Christ, sixteen hundred years since Constantine created his legions of "Christian citizens," two hundred years since forces began to conspire to bring down the coalition of church and state, Christians still don't quite know how to act as citizens of secular states. Jimmy Carter's Presidency should at least give us the chance to decide once for all. We may find that politics is indeed the way to put Christian principles into effect, the best way to help redeem the times. We may find that it is not, that we are more effective as outsiders, prophets.

The next few years should give us a good education. For it we have only to thank the thirty-ninth President, the Sunday school teacher from south Georgia, Jimmy Carter.